PYTHON CODING
AN EASY BOOK FOR
BEGINNERS

SECOND EDITION

Disclaimer

The software, programs, codes, or related documentation in this book are NOT designed nor intended for use (whether free or sold) as on-line control equipment in hazardous environments requiring fail-safe performance, such as, but not limited to, in the operation of nuclear facilities, aircraft navigation or communication systems, air traffic control, direct life support machines or weapons systems in which the failure of the hardware or software could lead directly to death, personal injury, or severe physical or environmental damage ("high risk activities").

The author(s) and publisher(s) take no responsibility for damages or injuries of any kind that may arise from the use or misuse of the software, programs, codes, or related documentation in this book.

The author(s) and publisher(s) specifically disclaim any express or implied warranty or fitness for high risk activities. The software, programs, codes, and related documentation are without warranty of any kind. The author(s) and publisher(s) expressly disclaim all other warranties, express or implied, including, but not limited to, the implied warranties of merchantability and fitness for a particular purpose.

Under no circumstances shall the author(s) and publisher(s) be liable for any incidental, special or consequential damages that result from the use or inability to use the software, programs, codes, or related documentation, even if he has been advised of the possibility of such damages.

Further, readers should be aware that Internet websites listed in this book may have changed or disappeared between when this book was written and when it is read.

Jason Latorilla

PYTHON CODING

AN EASY BOOK FOR BEGINNERS

SECOND EDITION

LESERATI CIRCLE PRESS   USA   EUROPE   ASIA   2022

If at first
you don't suceed
call it version 1.0

Notes to second edition

This second edition is the mass market version of
the first edition of the book. The difference in this
version is the grayscale and black & white print of
its contents.

This version is also registered at the
Library of Congress under
LCCN 2022907985.

Illustrations
by
Yzabella Latorilla

CONTENTS

	Introduction	10
Chapter 1	The Core Basics	39
Chapter 2	Numbers and Operators	54
Chapter 3	User Input, Strings, Lists	65
Chapter 4	if-else Statements	91
Chapter 5	Type Casting and Loops	110
Chapter 6	Turtle Graphics	119
Chapter 7	Functions and Arguments	153
Chapter 8	Modules and Challenges	163
	Chapter Solutions	173
	Functions and Methods Used in this Book	207
	References	216
	Acknowledgements	217
	Index	218
	About the Author	228

Python Programmers While Coding

Welcome to Python coding!

So, you want to learn computer coding? Well, you sure are a cool and curious person! Learning code is one of the best skills to have because it can help you solve problems and create awesome things! You can create games, algorithms, problem-solving code, and so much more programs! In short, code is built to translate human ideas into a language that machines can understand.

Code is the foundation of everything we love in the modern era. Innovations such as the laptop and the internet wouldn't have been possible without the creation and use of code. Learning code opens more opportunities for a future career and passion. Who knows, maybe one day you will become the next big innovator! Code is awesome because we can do anything, but how does it work?

Code is built around the concept of Input and Output. We give computers input, which is data or information provided from us humans, and we expect the computer to give us some output which can be anything ranging from a message to an action in a video game. We use a controller as input for a game to understand what action is to be done. This is the basis of the I/O concept.

Code is also founded on the principle of ones and zeros. These ones and zeros translate to True and False. A chain of ones and zeros commands a computer to do a task. To use an analogy, think of this scenario: If a button is clicked, it is currently True. Afterwards, it connects to other sets of True and False. If the button is true, then this part is true. Oh wait, it's true? Now this part is False. The chain eventually gives back some output. This idea of ones and zeros lay the foundation for computers today.

So yeah, coding is pretty awesome. We can do so many things thanks to the inventors of programming. Python is just one of many different languages of coding but is great for beginners to learn.

Are you ready to learn the Python language?

INTRODUCTION

Why Python?

Python is a great programming language to learn because it is easy to understand and can be used in many different ways. Python's syntax, or coding grammar, has a simple English sentence structure that makes it easy for young students to begin understanding programming logic. Python can be used on many different machines and run all sorts of tasks such as web development and data science. World-class companies like Google, Instagram, Spotify, and many others use Python programming.

Setting Up Python

To begin writing Python code, you will need to install Python to your computer. Don't worry about getting lost though! Screenshots are here to save the day! The step-by-step guide will help you set up Python.

If you are unsure how to do one of the steps, it is recommended that you ask a person who knows a lot about computers, such as a parent or friend, for help. These steps do require downloading and choosing the correct settings.

TIP:
Go to page 17 for the Windows guide or go to page 20 if you have already downloaded Python.

On macOS

1. On your Mac computer, start your preferred Internet browser app (Safari was used in this example) and locate the address bar.

2. In the address bar, type in the url: python.org/downloads OR https://www.python.org/downloads/

This is the Python website.

3. Hover on the **Downloads** tab and click on the **macOS** item.

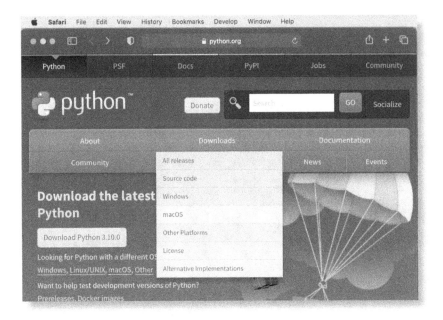

4. The Python website will automatically give you the correct version of Python to install. This version should be the latest version. At the time of writing this, the Python version available is 3.10.0 which explains why the screenshots show Python **3.10.0**.

5. Download the latest version, or the version that your computer can support, and a download should begin. In the example above, click on the "Download macOS 64-bit universal2 installer".

6. Once the download is finished, start the installer. Click on the **Downloads** icon on the upper right to show the downloaded installer package (a filename with ".pkg" at the end). Double click the file and the installer will start.

7. A window should pop up like the one below. Click the **Continue** button.

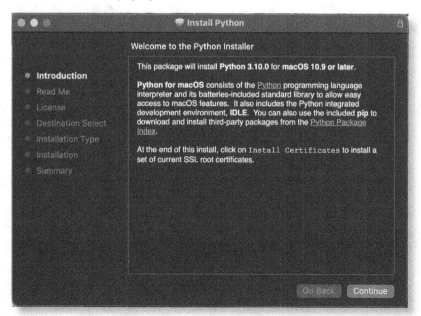

8. Afterwards, you'll see a window with important information which you can choose to read or not. Click the **Continue** button to proceed to the next step.

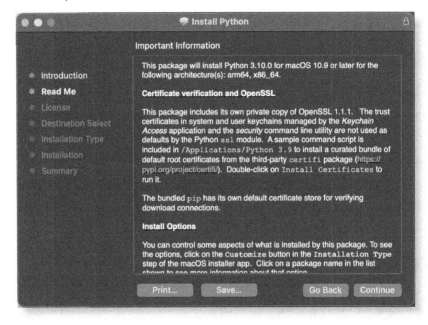

9. You'll then be presented the license information. Click the **Continue** button to move on.

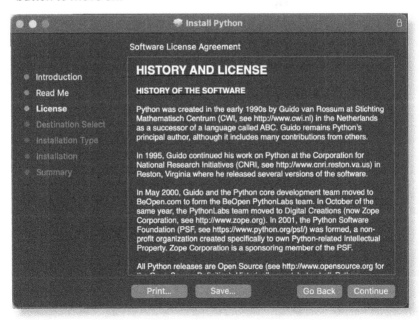

10. You'll be asked to agree to the terms of the software license agreement. Click the **Agree** button to continue.

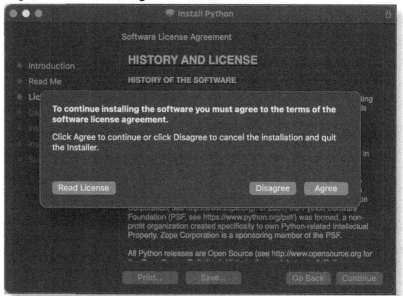

11. The final window should look like this. It shows the option to customize the location of the installation. If you don't know how to work file locations, don't worry about it. Click the **Install** button on the bottom of the window.

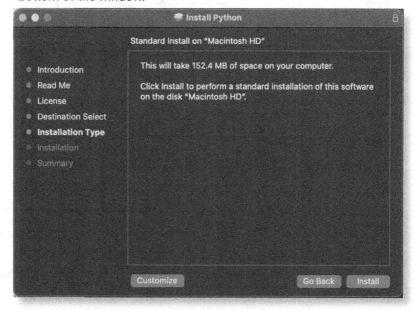

12. You may be asked to enter your username and password for your computer. MacOS sometimes asks for this whenever you install an app. If you don't see this pop up, you can skip this step.

13. Installation should begin. Wait for the installation to finish.

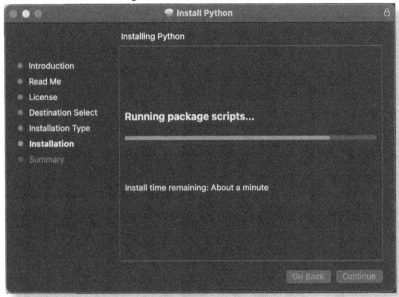

14. Once the installation is finished, you'll see a window that says Python was successfully installed. You can exit out of the window if you want.

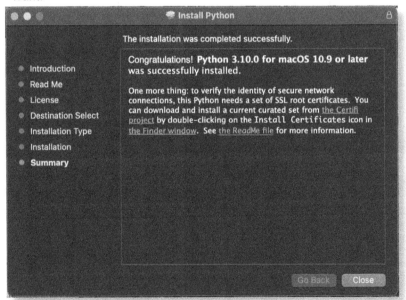

You've installed Python on your Mac. Now you're ready to begin coding!

On Windows

1. On your computer, open up your preferred Internet browser app and locate the address bar.

2. In the address bar, type in the url: python.org/downloads OR https://www.python.org/downloads/

3. Click the **Downloads** tab then click the Windows item.

4. The Python website will automatically show you the correct version of Python to install. This version should be the latest version. At the time of writing this book, the Python version available was 3.10.0 which explains why the screenshots show **Python 3.10.0**. Click the **Download** button.

5. A download will start and you might see it download at the bottom of your window.

6. Once the download has finished, double-click on the downloaded file to begin the installation. If a security warning does not pop up, don't worry about it and move on. If it does, go ahead and click the **Run** button.

7. Afterwards, another window should pop up. The window may say 64-bit or 32-bit depending on what you downloaded.

8. On the bottom of the window should be a checkbox labeled **Add Python (version) to PATH**. Make sure to check this if it hasn't already.

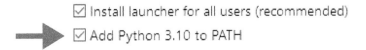

9. Click **Install Now** and Python should begin to install on your computer. The window should look something like this:

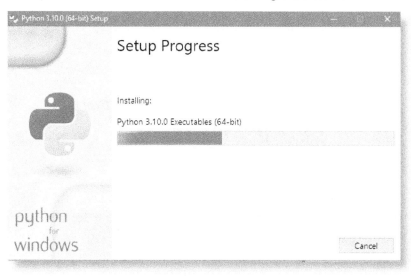

10. Once the installation is finished the final window should appear which says that your installation was successful. Go ahead and click the **Close** button on the bottom of the window.

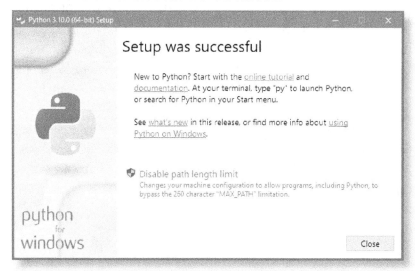

You've installed Python on Windows. It wasn't hard, was it?

Now onward you go, to learn how to begin coding!

Using IDLE

You may be wondering what IDLE is about. It is an application that is automatically downloaded when you download Python. Alongside IDLE comes other Python modules. You will use other Python modules by the end of the book.

IDLE is short for Integrated Development and Learning Environment. It is an IDE, or Integrated Development Environment, built for beginners like you to use Python. IDEs are useful because they come with syntax highlighting, autocomplete, and debugging. Syntax highlighting provides a visual representation of code, similar to how code is represented in this book.

Autocomplete helps finish lines of code because the IDE knows the syntax of the language that you are using. Debugging is incredibly useful to fix errors in code because IDEs highlight those errors. IDEs also help execute your code while other environments require more steps. IDLE is a great coding environment for beginners like you to learn Python.

You will be using IDLE to learn Python. You may switch coding environments once you finish this book or whenever you feel you are ready. To begin working with Python, you will need to open IDLE because opening Python files directly does not work.

TIP:
Go to page 23 for the Windows guide or go to page 24 to skip this guide entirely.

On macOS

1. Open the **Finder** app and navigate to **Applications**.

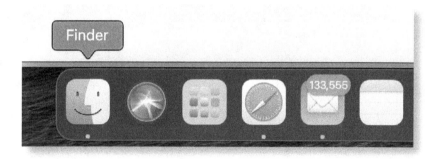

2. Find the **Python 3.10** folder and open it.

3. Double-click on the **IDLE** icon.

4. A window should pop up that looks like this:

YAY!

You've opened IDLE on Mac! Now you're ready to learn how to use it!

On Windows

1. Click on the Start Menu.

2. In the search bar, type "idle" and the result should be the app named **IDLE** with the version that you have installed.

3. Click on the **IDLE** app. A window should pop up that looks similar to this:

You've opened IDLE on Windows.
Now it's time to learn how to use IDLE.

Saying "Hi" to Python

Right at this moment, you can begin to write your first line of code in Python. Why? Because you've installed Python and IDLE on your computer! Hooray! Now it's time to say hi to Python.

When you start IDLE, the window that will always be opened is the **shell**. The shell is basically an interactive window where you can write short lines of Python code and see the result right away without having to write a long program. To check if you are actually in the shell, the name of the window should say "**IDLE Shell**" followed by the version number.

Now, let's say "Hi" to Python! Go ahead and type the following line:

```python
print("Hi, Python!")
```

This is what it should look like on Windows:

This is what it should look like on Mac:

Now press the **Enter** (or return) key on your keyboard. The following line will be shown.

> `Hi, Python!`

This is what it should look like on Windows:

```
IDLE Shell 3.10.0                                              □   ×
File  Edit  Shell  Debug  Options  Window  Help
     Python 3.10.0 (tags/v3.10.0:b494f59, Oct  4 2021, 19:00:18) [MSC v.1929 64 bit (
     AMD64)] on win32
     Type "help", "copyright", "credits" or "license()" for more information.
>>>  print("Hi, Python!")
     Hi, Python!
>>>  |

                                                              Ln: 5  Col: 0
```

This is what it should look like on Mac:

```
●  ●  ●                  IDLE Shell 3.10.0
     Python 3.10.0 (v3.10.0:b494f5935c, Oct  4 2021, 14:59:20) [
     Clang 12.0.5 (clang-1205.0.22.11)] on darwin
     Type "help", "copyright", "credits" or "license()" for more
     information.
>>>
>>>  print("Hi, Python!")
     Hi, Python!
>>>

                                                      Ln: 6  Col: 0
```

CONGRATS!

You've written your first line of Python code! Go show off to people your Python expertise! It's time to get ready to write amazing code!

Creating a File

As you progress through the book, the code and programs you write are going to get longer. One problem that occurs with using only the *IDLE Shell* to create programs is that you cannot have more than one line of code. Another problem is every time you open IDLE, you'd need to rewrite the code you previously had. These two problems can be solved by writing code in a Python file.

To create a file, first open *IDLE Shell* if you haven't already opened it.

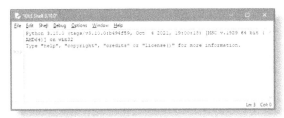

On the **Menu** bar click the **File** tab to open the tab's context menu.

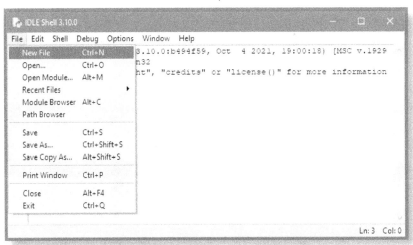

Click **New File**. A window should pop up similar to this:

This window is the editor where you can write Python programs with more than one line of code. Go ahead and type the greeting code from the previous example.

```
print("Hi, Python!")
```

Alright! Now you have a place where you can write longer programs!

Saving a File

While it's great and all that you can write longer programs, you still need a way to save the code.

1. First, navigate to the **Menu** bar on the file window. Click on the **File** tab.

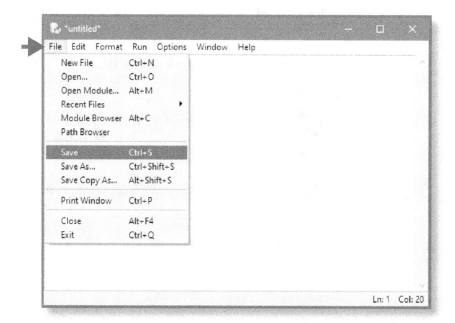

2. Click on the **Save** button.

3. A new window should appear. This window is where you save the file on your hard drive. On the bottom is a bar labeled **File name**:

Go ahead and give your file a name, any name that fits the purpose of your program.

4. Before you click **Save**, you should always organize where you keep your files. In this example a folder named **Python** was created in the Files directory. This way you always know where to find the Python files are whenever you need them. If you need someone to help you, now is the time to ask since it may get confusing at this step.

5. Finally, click **Save** and you're done!

Running a Program

Ok, so you have a line of code in a file. But how can you execute, or run, the code? Well that's quite easy! Just follow the steps below and you'll be a master at IDLE! (Skip to step 5 if you have the file already open.)

1. In the IDLE Shell, navigate to the menu bar and open the **File** tab.

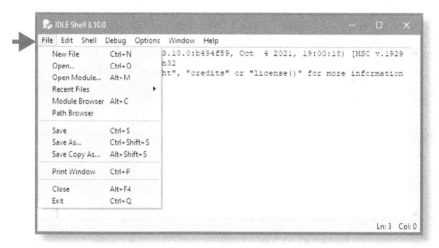

2. Click **Open...**

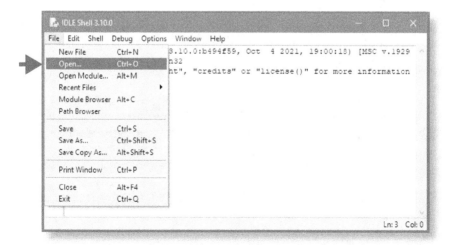

3. Your file directory should pop up. Look for the file that you created and select it. In this example the file is named "first_line.py". Then click **Open** on the bottom of the window. (*A Python file has ".py" at the end of its filename*)

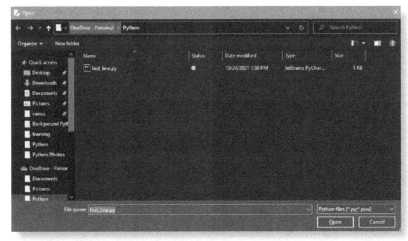

4. The file should open in the editor window showing your program.

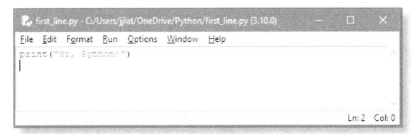

5. You can execute your program in two ways:

   a) Navigate to the menu bar on the editor's window and click the **Run** tab. Then click **Run Module**.

   b) Press the **F5** key on your keyboard.

Some coders prefer to press F5 since it saves some time from manually moving the mouse and clicking buttons.

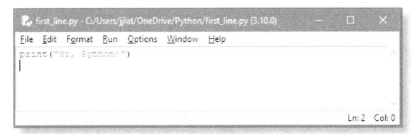

Keyboard Shortcuts

IDLE has its own keyboard shortcuts. If you don't know what keyboard shortcuts are, they are basic commands that you make using certain combinations of keys on your keyboard. Here is a list of helpful shortcuts that can be used while you write your Python code.

TIP: **Ctrl** is short for the Control key. For Mac: Ctrl = command.

Ctrl + S	This is the standard save shortcut. Pressing both keys will save your file.
Ctrl + C	The standard copy shortcut. Any text highlighted using your mouse will be copied. To do this, click and hold your left mouse button (LMB) and drag your cursor across the text you want to highlight. Afterwards, do Ctrl +C to copy the text.
Ctrl + V	The standard paste shortcut. Using this shortcut will paste any text you copied to where you are typing.
Ctrl + X	This shortcut allows you to cut out text but also copy it. Similar to the Ctrl +C shortcut but cuts out, or deletes, the highlighted text. It can be pasted using Ctrl +P.
Ctrl + Z	This shortcut performs an undo action. For example, if you accidentally deleted some code, using this shortcut will restore the code. This shortcut can be used multiple times to reverse an action.
Ctrl +SHIFT+ Z	This shortcut performs a redo action. It's basically the opposite of the undo shortcut. It can also be used multiple times to redo an action.
Ctrl + A	This shortcut will select all text. It will highlight all code/text in a window. It's good for copying entire programs.
Ctrl + N	Ctrl +N: This shortcut creates a new file and opens it.

EXTRA LEARNING: RECENT FILES

This is your first look at Extra Learning sections. These sections pop up randomly around each chapter. Extra learning sections provide additional content on a topic and can give helpful tips or background information. This extra learning is about using recent files.

Sometimes searching for a file can get hard, especially when you create more and more programs as you learn. Luckily, IDLE has a feature where you can open a recently opened file. Recent files are based on when you opened them in a chronological order. The most recent file you opened will be the first on the list. This helps find files that you may have opened an hour ago or even a couple days ago. It's especially useful when you are working on a program everyday.

To find your recent files, simply go to the **File** tab and navigate to **Recent Files**. Hovering your cursor over **Recent Files** will open another context menu which will show you a list of your recently opened files.

This is how it looks like:

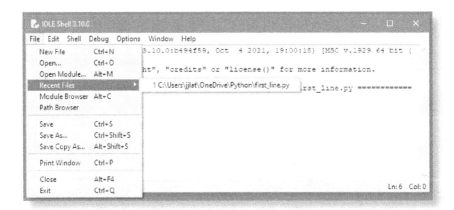

The Book Guide

A guide to using this book properly and to make coder's life easier

Wow, a book guide! This guide is a walkthrough to using the book properly. Below is an imitation of the beginning of a chapter. The next page consists of explanations for the content of the book pages.

TIP: If you want to dive into actual coding right away, go to page 39.

Chapter Heading

Chapter Subheading

Topic Heading

Subtopic Heading

Main Text Heading

Main Text

Sample text. Buda-Pesth seems a wonderful place, from the glimpse which I got of it from the train and the little I could walk through the streets. I feared to go very far from the station, as we had arrived late and would start as near the correct time as possible. All day long we seemed to dawdle through a country which was full of beauty of every kind. Sometimes we saw little towns or castles on the top of steep hills such as we see in old missals; sometimes we ran by rivers and streams which seemed from the wide stony margin on each side of them to be subject to great floods. It takes a lot of water, and running strong, to sweep the outside edge of a river clear.

```
print("Hello, World!")
Hello, World!
```

The impression I had was that we were leaving the West and entering the East; the most western of splendid bridges over the Danube, which is here of noble width and depth, took us among the traditions of Turkish rule.

Sample Text

It seems to me that the further east you go the more unpunctual are the trains. What ought they to be in China? I find that the district he named is in the extreme east of the country, just on the borders of three states, Transylvania, Moldavia, and Bukovina, in the midst of the Carpathian mountains; one of the wildest and least known portions of Europe.

Headings

In this book there are six types of headings, beginning from largest to smallest: chapter heading, chapter subheading, topic heading, subtopic heading, main text heading, and the main text (main text is not a heading but the actual content being taught.)

Chapter Heading
The chapter heading consists of the chapter's title and number. It is within a faint green box along with a subheading.

Chapter Subheading
The chapter subheading is below the chapter heading. It is usually called *"What To Expect"* where it contains more context about the detail in the chapter. Shown below is an example of a chapter heading:

Chapter 1

The Core Basics: print(), Syntax, Data Types, Variables, and more

What to Expect: Using print(), comments, variables, data types and F-strings

Topic Heading

The topic heading is the heading for a major topic in a chapter. Topic headings are also based on the contents listed in the chapter heading/ subheading. This heading are indicated with a green line below the text as shown below:

Hello, World!

Subtopic Heading
The subtopic heading falls under topic headings. Subtopics are branched off from the main topic. This means that there can be multiple subtopics. Subtopic headings are indicated with one green line below the text:

print()

Main Text Heading

The main text heading divides the content in a topic. For example:

Syntax on Escape Characters and Multilines

Yes! More Syntax! It's very important!

Main Text

The main text is the content of the chapter/topic. It is the explanations and examples for each topic or visual representation. The main text is the smallest text that is not in bold. In addition to the main text some words or phrases will be italicized. Italicized text represents key concepts or vocabulary words. Here is an example:

In the previous function, we used *greet* as our name for the function.

To finish, some words can be colored to identify keywords in code. Here is an example:

The *print*() function can take in one or more parameters.

Screenshots

This book uses screenshots to show code or what the user should see. Screenshots are mostly used in chapters 1 and 6, but are sometimes shown in chapter reviews or in other chapters.

Screenshots are also used as a visual guide to downloading and setting up Python and IDLE, so you've already seen how screenshots are shown in this book. Anyway, here's one:

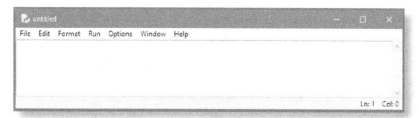

Not all screenshots will have the same border width.
Some may be bigger or smaller.

Code Tables

Code shown in this book are mostly represented through sections that the author happily coined as code tables. Code tables are easily distinguishable from the main text. Code tables are basically boxes with text inside it. They have a light grey background with a color bar on the left side of the code. Here's an example of a code table:

```python
def add(int_one, int_two):
        final_num = int_one + int_two
        return final_num
```

Code, as you can see, is the text within the table. On the left side there is a color coded bar. It is green in this example. The color represents the type of code being represented in the book (Note that *"type of code"* is not a Python term and only used here for visual representation). Below is a table of the color bar color coding.

Color	Name	Purpose
Green	Sample Code	*Indicates examples of code**
Purple	Lesson Code	*Code that is directly being changed in a chapter/ topic***
Blue	Output	*Indicates the output text*
Yellow	File Code	*Code that is written in a file*
Red	Exercise/Challenge Code	*Examples of Code in exercises or challenges*
Dark gray	Other Code	*Code that does not fit into any of the categories above*

* This kind of code is often used to represent concepts in a chapter.

** The meaning of "directly being changed" is that it is code formed through steps in a process which means, in even more simpler terms, the full length of the code is not exactly shown.

Here is an example of a code table with multiple color coded bars.

```
print("Hi, Python!")
Hi, Python!
print("Say Hello to the world!")
Say Hello to the world!
```

Color Coding of Code

You may have noticed that the code in the tables are colored. All of the code that is not in a screenshot follows a color coding which distinguishes the elements and words in code. IDLE uses color to differentiate between keywords such as strings, comments, functions and booleans but some code such as variables and integers do not have a unique color.

The book's color code is similar to IDLE with a few changes and extra keywords represented. Below is a table of the keyword colors.

Color	Type of Code	Example
Red	Comments	#This is a comment
Green	Strings	"Hello, World!"
Orange/Yellow*	Keywords and Booleans	def, for, in, while, return, True, False
Blue	Functions, Objects , Logical Operators	greet() and, or, not
Black	Syntax and Operators	, [] () {} : = - = == += etc
Purple	Python In-Built Functions	print() input() range() type() int() str() float()
Light Pink	Variables	myVariable = "Hi!"
Light Blue	Integers and Floats	201, 97.8
Dark Blue	Output Text	Hello, World!

Here is an example of some code:

```
password = "0123456789"
response = "Correct!"
answer = ""
while answer != password:
        name = input("What is the password? ")
print(response)
```

Chapter Quick Reviews

At the end of each chapter is an overview of the chapter. These reviews are called "Chapter Quick Reviews", obviously. Chapter reviews list the main concepts of each section and highlight the important takeaways. These reviews are especially helpful to remember definitions of vocabulary and use of keywords.

Here is an example of a Chapter Review:

Chapter 1 Quick Review

print() is a function that outputs text.

Strings are text. That's literally it.

Comments help organize and label code.

Comments can disable a line of code.

Syntax is important to code. It is the grammar for your code. If you don't follow it, you're going to be slapped with errors that you probably don't even understand.

Escape characters can add quotes into a string and create a multiline sentence.

A **data type** holds a type of information. You have learned the basics of **strings** and **integers**.

WooHo!

You've completed the Introduction Section! You've set up Python, learned how to use IDLE, and the basic features of this book. You are ready to begin your Python coding career!!

Chapter 1

The Core Basics: print(), Syntax, Data Types, Variables, and more

What to Expect: Using print(), comments, variables, data types and F-strings

print()

When you first set up Python and used IDLE, your first line of code may have looked liked this:

```
● ● ●                    *IDLE Shell 3.10.0*
Python 3.10.0 (v3.10.0:b494f5935c, Oct  4 2021, 14:59:20) [
Clang 12.0.5 (clang-1205.0.22.11)] on darwin
Type "help", "copyright", "credits" or "license()" for more
information.
>>> print("Hi, Python"!)

                                          Ln: 3  Col: 20
```

Or you tried to stay cool and did `print("sup world")` which is completely fine and totally awesome. But what does this line of code even mean anyway?

First, strip the code to the bare bones. Remove the text in quotations and ignore it for now. You will be left with print(). This code is a Python built-in function. It is called *"Python built-in"* because you will be making your own functions in later chapters.

A function is basically telling the computer to do a specific task for you. That task is to give back some output. A function can be easily recognized with its pair of parentheses. This set of parentheses is also where you give the function parameters, or information that you pass over to a function. The *print()* function can take one or more parameters and it will then tell the computer to output the parameters passed to it, for example "Hello, World!"

A **string** is a data type which represents text including punctuation, numbers, and spaces. Strings are written within a pair of double-quotation marks and are often shown in green color.

For now, you will be using the *print()* function and strings to create some cool text! Since you know the basics, why not try it out? Go ahead and print some text!

Here's an example:

```
print("Hello, World!")
Hello, World!
print("My name is Jason")
My name is Jason
print("I like to code!")
I like to code!
```

Here's the example in IDLE Shell on Mac:

```
IDLE Shell 3.10.0
Python 3.10.0 (v3.10.0:b494f5935c, Oct  4 2021, 14:59:20) [Clang 12.0.5
(clang-1205.0.22.11)] on darwin
Type "help", "copyright", "credits" or "license()" for more information.
>>>
>>> print("Hello, World!")
Hello, World!
>>> print("My name is Jason")
My name is Jason
>>> print("I like to code!")
I like to code!
>>>
                                                              Ln: 10  Col: 0
```

Important note:
After chapter 1 most screenshots will be shown on a Mac version.

Comments

One important feature in coding that will be shown throughout this entire book is comments. Comments are very useful for code. They help explain parts of your code to anyone who'd like to read it. This is what a comment looks like:

```
#Hi there! This is a comment!
print("This is not a comment!")
```

On Mac:

```
*IDLE Shell 3.10.0*
Python 3.10.0 (v3.10.0:b494f5935c, Oct  4 2021, 14:59:20) [C
lang 12.0.5 (clang-1205.0.22.11)] on darwin
Type "help", "copyright", "credits" or "license()" for more
information.
>>>
>>> #Hi there! This is a comment!
>>> print("This is not a comment!")


                                                Ln: 5  Col: 32
```

On Windows:

```
*IDLE Shell 3.10.0*                              —    □    ×
File  Edit  Shell  Debug  Options  Window  Help
Python 3.10.0 (tags/v3.10.0:b494f59, Oct  4 2021, 19:00:18)
[MSC v.1929 64 bit (AMD64)] on win32
Type "help", "copyright", "credits" or "license()" for more
information.
>>> #Hi There! This is a comment!
>>> print("This is not a comment!")

                                                Ln: 4  Col: 31
```

Comments can be created with a single hashtag (#). Any text after the hashtag will be in a distinct red font color. This allows spaces and special characters to be in hashtags because comments do not affect code in any way. This means that you can also "disable" lines of code.

Here is a basic example:

```
#print("Don't print me!")
print("Hello, World!")
```

Disabling lines of code can be useful for you in the future. Why? Because it can be used in a process called **debugging**, or looking for errors and fixing them.

Comments are also useful for labeling parts of code, especially for long programs.

Here is an example:

```
#Check player's score
if firstPlayerScore > secondPlayerScore:
    #print winner's name
    print(f"{firstPlayerName} wins!")

elif firstPlayerScore < secondPlayerScore:
    print(f"{secondPlayerName} wins!")

else:
    #if scores are equal, print tie
    print("It's a tie!")
```

Syntax

Have you received an error in your code yet? No? Then type this:

```python
print("haha im cool i use "quotes" in this")
```

Now, did your computer tell you this?

```
IDLE Shell 3.10.0
Python 3.10.0 (v3.10.0:b494f5935c, Oct  4 2021, 14:59:20) [Clang 12.0.5
(clang-1205.0.22.11)] on darwin
Type "help", "copyright", "credits" or "license()" for more information.
>>>
>>> print(▮haha im cool i use "quotes" in this")
SyntaxError: invalid syntax. Perhaps you forgot a comma?
>>> |
                                                        Ln: 6  Col: 0
```

Congratulations! You received your first error (unless you messed up somehow beforehand)! Why am I praising you for getting an error? Well, because it's the error that you should learn!

The error you received:

```
SyntaxError: invalid syntax. Perhaps you forgot a comma?
```

It is asking if you perhaps "forgot a comma." For now, ignore that part and focus on the error itself, SyntaxError: invalid syntax. What is syntax, and if you know some other coding languages, what is Python syntax?

Syntax is basically ground rules that define how Python will read and execute code. You can also say that syntax is grammar for not only the Python language, but for all computer languages.

So why did you get a syntax error? It wasn't that your English was wrong. The computer got confused because you have either mixed up the quotation marks or missed some characters that are required.

Here's what's happening. Python reads the sample code from left to right. When it detects the first quotation mark, it assumes that everything after that quotation mark is a string. So it reads the rest of the code as a string until it reaches the second quotation mark and completes the string.

In the example above Python reads it as *"haha im cool i use"* but when it encounters the following word 'quotes', it is not within the quotation marks and Python returns the error "invalid syntax". You might insist that it is correct because you have used quotation marks within the string. That is exactly the reason for the error.

Python reads the characters within the first pair of quotation marks as a string and thinks the following word *'quotes'* is a variable with wrong syntax. If you were to correct the syntax, you would need to add a comma (,) both after the first string and after the word *'quotes'*. The correct syntax would look like this:

```
print("haha im cool i use", quotes, "in this")
```

But that's not the output that you wanted since you want the actual quotation mark (") to be part of the string. So, how do you fix that? Simple. Instead of using double quotation marks (") in the beginning and end of the string, you use single quote marks ('). It should look like this:

```
print('haha im cool i use"quotes" in this')
```

Boom! Fixed! You are a genius. Python now reads all the characters (including the double quote marks) within the single quotes as a string. This is also a good time to talk about how quotation marks are used in this book. Double quotes are used for sentences and long texts. Single quotes are used for very short strings such as single words or letters.

Here is a couple of examples:

Double Quotes:

```
player_choice = input("Where do you want to go next?")
```

Single Quotes:

```
if player_choice == 'a':
```

Syntax on Escape Characters and Multilines

Yes! More Syntax! It's very important!

Escape characters are basically the '\' or *backslash* and '/' or *forward slash*. They are used in strings to help print out what you want in that string. Have a look!

```
print("So cool! I can use \"quotes\" in this string!")
```

The backslashes help Python identify that the double quote marks are part of the string.

Now with the knowledge you have with escape characters, you can also use them to print multiple lines of text. What are they? Well it's exactly what they are called! Text that spans multiple lines. Here is an example:

This

Is

A

Multi

Line

Sentence

So how can you print such a sentence that way? Well here's how! You add the characters **\n** (backslash followed by the small letter **n**) in front of every word.

```python
print("This \nIs \nA \nMulti \nLine \nSentence")
```

The '**\n**' tells Python to print the text on a new line. Why not try it out? You could probably even print a complete poem!

Sometimes it can be hard to read a sentence like that, so there is another way to make multiline sentences! You add three double quotes (" " ") together on both ends of the string. Here's how it should look:

```python
print("""
This
Is
A
Multi
Line
Sentence
""")
```

This is what it looks like in IDLE shell:

```
●  ●  ●                    IDLE Shell 3.10.0
      Python 3.10.0 (v3.10.0:b494f5935c, Oct  4 2021, 14:59:20) [Clang 12.0.5
      (clang-1205.0.22.11)] on darwin
      Type "help", "copyright", "credits" or "license()" for more information.
>>>
>>>  print("""
...  This
...  Is
...  A
...  Multi
...  Line
...  Sentence
...  """)

      This
      Is
      A
      Multi
      Line
      Sentence

>>>  |
                                                              Ln: 20  Col: 0
```

There is a lot more about syntax but to make it short and easy you will learn the syntax along the way by simply following what to type. You will know how to use colons, apostrophes, parenthesis, upper and lowercase, and much more.

Data Types

Data types are strings, integers, booleans, lists, and more. They store different types of information. What you have learned up to this point is the string data type.

So it's time to get to know integers. Integers are whole numbers either negative or positive. You can assign an integer number to a variable by typing the following:

```
my_lucky_number = 10
print(my_lucky_number)
10
```

So far so good! Now type the following:

```
my_lucky_number = 10
print(type(my_lucky_number))
```

Wait, what is type()? It's a function used to identify a variable's data type. In this case Python prints out the following:

       <class 'int'>

This means that the variable *"my_lucky_number"* is an integer data type. How about you try the following:

```
random_num = "234"
print(type(random_num))
```

Did you get <class 'str'>?

Well, that means the variable *"random_num"* is a string data type!

This is the reason why you don't enclose numbers with quotation marks because they make Python assume it was a string.

You will get more in depth with integers in later chapters.

Variables

Variables are absolutely important to coding. It is a data type that stores information. This is an example of what a variable looks like:

```
my_name = 'Jason'
```

The variable here is *"my_name"* which holds the information 'Jason'. Variables are created using a special symbol called assignment operator. The assignment operator is the equal sign = . After the assignment operator you add in any information you want. You can later use this information in different parts of the code and this information can be changed or added on to. But more on that later. Here, you can use variables to simplify your code. Try this:

```
#the variable
my_name = 'Jason'
#print the variable
print(my_name)
Jason
```

Awesome, right? What is happening here is that you are assigning the information 'Jason' in the variable *"my_name"*. The *print()* function is used to print out the information contained in the variable *"my_name"*.

Why can't you use quotation marks to print the variable? Because the variable *"my_name"* itself is not a string! You want Python to know that *"my_name"* is a variable and print out what's stored in the variable. Otherwise, the following happens:

```
my_name = 'Jason'
print("my_name")
my_name
```

It printed the word my_name not the word Jason

Variable Do's and Don'ts

Variables can't start with a number. Check it out yourself.

```
100_days = 100
SyntaxError: invalid decimal literal
```

See? Python gets confused by the number at the start of the variable's name.

Variables Need The Same Styling

Yes, they are all branded too. What is meant by this is that you need to stick to a format that's readable and used consistently for all variables. Here are some examples:

camelCase:

The first word of the variable is lowercase and the rest of the words start with an uppercase. There are no underscores.
Example: timeUntilDay

PascalCase:

All words in the variable start with an uppercase, without underscores.
Example: BankMoney

snake_case:

Underscores are used for spacing between words.
Example: country_of_origin

Good variables have meaningful names. It should give you an idea about what kind of information is contained in the variable. Examples are:

```python
tree = 'oak'
colorOfHouse = 'white'
books_owned = 23
```

These are good ways to keep your code organized and clean.

Bad variable names are either hard to read or too vague about what kind of information is stored in the variable. Examples are:

```
q = False
doc_ap = "Tuesday"
ctOR = 'Asia'
fAvOrItE_FoOd = 'chicken'
```

Using Variable in Strings

Up to this point you have used variables to store information and then print it. But what if you want it to print differently? What if you want to have a part of the string be a variable? Here is an example of printing a string without a variable:

```
print("Hello there, Jason!")
```

How can you change the word "Jason" into a variable that you can assign any name? What if you want the name "Mike" or "Player3409"? You can't just type the variable's name to replace "Jason" in the string, it just won't work!

Well, here's the solution:

```
#assign the information to the variable
my_name = "Mike"
#print the string and content of variable
print("Hi there, " + my_name )
```

Did it print out "Hi there, Mike"? If so, then you did it correctly! This is called **concatenation string**, where you use the addition symbol **+** (plus symbol) to combine words and variables together in a string. You will learn more about this in later chapters.

In the example above, try changing the name to something else and run the code. This will be useful for coding games in the future.

Formatted String Literals

Wow! A complex and fancy name for something so simple! Formatted String Literals, or F-strings for short, is another way of using variables in strings. To put it simply, it literally just describes the letter 'f'.

This is what an F-string looks like:

```
#variable for my favorite drink
my_drink = 'water'
print(f"My favorite drink is {my_drink}")
```

F-strings are made by typing the letter ' f ' just before the quotation marks in the string. This tells Python that you want to make an F-String. Then you type in the sentence including the variable, but you type braces {} around the variable. Python reads this and knows that this is the variable you want to be in the string.

F-strings are a great way of making it easy to add variables into a string. Just look at the difference when using multiple variables within the string:

Not an F-string

```
print("Hi, my name is "+my_name+". I love to "+my_hobby+"everyday!")
```

This is an F-string

```
print(f"Hi, my name is {my_name}. I love to {my_hobby} everyday!")
```

There are certain times when you don't want to use an F-String, but using it in long strings helps keep the code clean.

CONGRATULATIONS!

You've just completed chapter 1! It's time to review what you learned.

Chapter 1 Quick Review

print() is a function that outputs text.

Strings are text. That's literally it.

Comments help organize and label code.

Comments can disable a line of code.

Syntax is important to code. It is the grammar for your code. If you don't follow it, you're going to be slapped with errors that you probably don't even understand.

Escape characters can add quotes into a string and create a multiline sentence.

A **data type** holds a type of information. You have learned the basics of **strings** and **integers**.

Variables also have naming rules that you don't need to follow but should.

F-string-s, or Formatted String Literals, allow variables to be in a string.

Chapter 1 Exercises

At the end of every chapter, there will be exercises to improve what you have learned. Doing these exercises is the best way to look back into the chapter and go step-by-step to fully understand coding.

Exercise #1 - Greet yourself
In this exercise, you want to greet yourself using a string as the parameter.
Here is a code for you: print(#You finish the rest!

Exercise #2 - Helping a friend?
In this exercise, you need to help a friend fix his coding. Can you fix it so that it runs properly?

```
name = Roger
country = Canada
favorite_food = Pancakes
print("Hi, my name is name, I am from country and my favorite
food is favorite_food!")
```

Exercise #3 - Which code works?

In this exercise, you need to create a file (*see page 26 if you have forgotten how to*) and copy the code shown below into the file. Run the code and see which lines are correct. But you want to keep the incorrect lines instead of deleting them. How to do that? You can also label the lines of code at the same.

```
a = "Person"
print("a")
a = "Person"
print(a)
```

Exercise #4 - Haiku?

In this exercise, you need to make a haiku using multiline sentences. Here is a sample haiku. You make your own.

```
I don't know how to
Make a haiku okay? See,
I am bad at this
```

Exercise #5 - Variables and variables?

In this exercise, make a variable for your first name and another variable for your last name. Create a variable that combines the first two variables so that when you print the variable, it prints out your full name.
Sample code:

```
first_name = 'Mohammad'
last_name = 'Ali'
full_name = #Fill This In!
print(full_name)
```

Exercise #6 - Mad Libs?

In this exercise, you will create your own mad libs story. Mad libs is a game where you need to fill in the blanks with words to complete the story. You can do this by using variables and a variable that holds your story. Here is a sample code:

```
story = f"""
        There once lived a {animal} who liked to {hobby}.
        This {animal} liked to eat {food}.
        One day, the {animal} {verb1} to {place}.
        There the {animal} {verb2} for {number} hours.
        """
```

Chapter 2

Numbers and Operators

You will learn Numeric Types, different types of Operators, and Boolean Logic

Now we're talking numbers! Don't worry about using a calculator though because Python will do the work for you, although coding a calculator program would be a nice challenge. This chapter is vital to learn to understand later chapters.

Numeric Types

To start off this chapter, you need to learn Python's numeric types. Numeric types help you to count objects, store data of items, perform mathematical operations and more! Python's two main numeric types are *integers* and *floating point numbers*. Up to this point you have known the integer type.

Integers are whole numbers that are either positive or negative. Floating point numbers, or *floats* for short, are either positive or negative and have one or more decimals. Here's some examples:

Integers

```
score = 100
apples = 23
money = -9999999
```

Floats

```
average = 97.8
result = 3.392
the_pi = 3.14159
```

Floats look like decimal numbers but they are not exactly the same. Floats are used in mathematical operations where precise calculations are needed, most often in math or science.

Operators

In coding, operators are symbols used to perform operations on variables or values. The variables or values being used with an operator are called *operands*. Keep these terms in mind, you will use them in later chapters. There are different types of operators. These are:

arithmetic	**assignment**	**comparison**
logical identity	**membership**	**bitwise**

That's a lot to learn, but don't worry about it too much at this time. In this chapter, you will learn arithmetic, assignment, comparison and logical operators. In later chapters you will learn comparison, identity and membership operators. However, bitwise operators are not discussed in this book but doing extra research on your own about it can help improve your coding skill.

Arithmetic Operators

Arithmetic, or simply math, operators are used to perform basic math operations. Here is a cool chart of all the arithmetic operators you need to know.

Operator	Name	Objective	Example
+	Addition	Adds two values together	1 + 1
-	Subtraction	Subtracts one value from another	2 - 2
__*__	Multiplication	Multiplies two values together	4 * 5
/	Division	Divides one value by another. Some results can be floats.	5 / 2 Result = 2.5
%	Modulus	Divides one value by another and gives the remainder.	10 % 7 Result = 3
//	Floor Division	Divides one value by another. If the result is a float it will round it.	8 // 3 Result = 3
**	Exponentiation	Raises one value to the power of another value	3 ** 6 Result = 729

Go ahead and try them! You can even use variables to represent numbers. Here's one example:

```
a - 3
b - 2
a + b
```

If you were to combine these operators, Python follows the standard order of operations. A good way to remember the standard order of operations is to use the word **PEMDAS**. It means Parentheses, Exponentiation, Multiplication, Division, Addition, Subtraction.

Assignment Operators

Basically, assignment operators are used to assign values to variables. Remember chapter 1 where you learned about variables? You had already used an assignment operator ---- the equal operator **=** .

Here is a table of the assignment operators you can use:

Operator	Objective	Example
=	Assigns value from right operand to left side operand	a = b
+=	Adds right operand to left operand and assigns result to left operand	a += b a = a + b
-=	Subtracts right operand from left operand and assigns result to left operand	a -= b a = a - b
*=	Multiplies right operand with left operand and assigns result to left operand	a *= b a = a * b
/=	Divides left operand with right operand and assigns result to left operand	a /= b a = a /b
%=	Takes Modulus of both operands and assigns result to left operand	a %= b a = a % b
//=	Performs floor division on both operands and assigns result to left operand	a //= b a = a // b
**=	Performs exponentiation of left operand using right operand as the power and assigns result to left operand	a **= b a = a ** b

*** The red colored code is the equivalent code

In other words: What these operators do is math operations with both operands and the result is assigned to the left operand. Here is a visual explanation:

> a is the left operand, **b** is the right operand
> ## a += b
> += will do (**a** + **b**) and assign the result to a

Makes sense, right? This can be useful when you want to increment, or add to, a value repeatedly. On the opposite you can also decrement, or subtract from, a value repeatedly. One possible use of this is in writing a code for a scoring system.

Comparison Operators

Comparison operators are used to compare values or variables. You will be using a lot of comparison operators to handle values. When you compare two values using a comparison operator, it results in either True or False value. These true and false values are called Booleans. Booleans help make decisions in our code. You will use Booleans more in the next chapter. You will learn the six main comparison operators in this chapter.

Greater Than (>)

The *greater than* operator compares the left operand with the right operand and determines if the left operand is greater, or bigger in value, than the right operand. If it is, the result is True. Otherwise, if the left operand is less than the right operand, the result is False.

Here's a couple of examples:

```
15 > 6
True

12 > 20
False
```

Simple, right? You can go ahead and try out a few more.

Now this operator is great for comparing values, but you can also be more advanced and do math operations with the operands then check if the result of one operation is greater than the result of the other operation.

You can also use it to compare variables.

```
18 + 2 > 4 * 4
True

number = 23
30 - 5 > 6 + number
False
```

Less Than (<)

The *less than* operator is the opposite of the *greater than* operator. It compares the left operand with the right operand and determines if the right operand is greater than the left operand.

Here's a couple of examples:

```
23 < 4
False
4 < 5
True
```

And it can also be used to compare results and variables.

```
5 + 3 < 50 / 2
True
number = 23
other_num = 53
number < other_num
True
```

Greater Than or Equal to (>=)

Now this operator is a little bit more complicated. The *greater than or equal to* operator checks the left operand if it is greater than OR equal to the right operand. The result will be *true* if the left operand is either greater or equal to the value of the right operand.

Here's a couple of examples:

```
41 >= 6
True
15 >= 15
True
```

And it can also be used with math operations and variables.

```
number = 3
other_num = 6 - 3
number >= other_num
True
```

Less Than or Equal To (<=)

It is literally the opposite of the *greater than or equal to* operator. This operator checks if the left operand is less than the right operand or if the left operand is equal to the right operand.

Here's a couple of examples:

```
52 <= 300
True
20.5 <= 20
False
```

And you know how it goes, it also works with math operations and variables but since you already understand that concept you don't really need an example. Here's one anyway if you want it.

```
20+25 <= 60 - 15
True
number = 56
other_num = 12
number <= other_num
False
```

Equal to (==)

This operator is very simple. The *equal to* operator checks if both operands have the same value. The reason why it is a double-equals symbol == is because the equals symbol by itself = is already reserved as an assignment operator.

Here's a few examples.

```
2 + 2 == 5 + 5
False
variable1 = 54 + 1
variable2 = 55
variable1 == variable2
True
```

The *equal to* operator is most commonly used in *if, else* statements which you will learn in chapter 4. So keep that in mind since it is important to syntax!

Not Equal To (!=)

This is the last comparison operator you will learn. The *not equal to* operator checks if the left operand is not equal to the right operand. It is also commonly used in *if, else* statements.
Here are some examples:

```
34 != 34
False

2 + 5 != 4 - 2
True
variable1 = 54 + 1
variable2 = 50
variable1 != variable2
True
```

Here's what that looks like on IDLE shell.

```
IDLE Shell 3.10.0
>>>
>>> 34 != 34
    False
>>> 2 + 5 != 4 - 2
    True
>>> variable1 = 54 + 1
>>> variable2 = 50
>>> variable1 != variable2
    True
>>>
>>>
                                          Ln: 18  Col: 0
```

Logical Operators

Logical operators are used to determine *True* or *False* statements. The logical operators are **and**, **or**, and **not**.

and operator

The and operator combines two values and checks if both are true. You can use this operator when the program should only proceed when both conditions are met (or true).
Here's some examples:

```
variable1 = True
variable2 = True
variable1 and variable2
True
```

If one or both variables is false the result is always False.

```
variable1 = False
variable2 = True
variable1 and variable2
False
```

or operator

The or operator checks if one value is true. You can use this operator when the code needs at least one condition met (or true) for the program to proceed.

Here's an example:

```
variable1 = True
variable2 = False
variable1 or variable2
True
```

not operator

The not operator inverts the logical value of a variable without changing the variable. This is great to use in *if, else* statements where the code needs the logical value to be true in order for the program to proceed. Here's some examples:

```
variable = False
not variable
True
variable = True
not variable
False
```

Combining Operators

Here you are going to learn a little more about using the different types of operators that you just learned. You can combine these operators to solve complex coding problems. When you first learned about arithmetic operators, you learned that you can combine arithmetic operators together. But what you see here is combining different types of operators. Here is an example:

```
var1 and var2 != var3
```

You can see the logical operator and with the comparison operator != (*not equal to*). We often combine these operators to compare one condition to a second or multiple conditions. Here is another example:

```
var1 or var2 or var3 or var4 or var5 == var6
```

It may seem strange using excessive **or** operators but you just might have to do it for a particular coding solution.

CONGRATULATIONS!

You've just completed chapter 2! Now, time to review what you learned.

Chapter 2 Quick Review

Integers and **Floats** are the two main numeric types in Python.

Integers are whole numbers, either positive or negative.

Floats (floating point numbers) are numbers that have decimals.

Operators are symbols used to perform operations on variables or values. The types of operators are *arithmetic, assignment, comparison, logical, identity, membership* and *bitwise*.

Arithmetic Operators perform math operations. Arithmetic operators follow the standard order of operations (PEMDAS).

Comparison Operators compare two operands or values. These operators are *greater than, less than, greater than or equal to, less than or equal to, equal to,* and *not equal to*.

Logical Operators are used to determine *True* or *False* statements. These operators are *and, or,* and *not*.

We can combine different operators to solve complex coding problems.

In the next chapter, you will learn about Python's arrays, aka lists and more!

Chapter 2 Exercises

Exercise #1 - **Basic Greeting**

In this exercise, you want to print out a greeting that tells who you are and what your age is. For this, use two variables to represent your name and age. Use an arithmetic operator that adds up your age.

Sample code:

```
name = "Harry Potluck"
age = #Use an arithmetic operator!
print(#Print out your greeting!)
```

Sample output:

Hey there! My name is Harry Potluck and I am 142 years old!

Exercise #2 - The Mysterious Float

In this exercise, you need a variable that will hold the value of zero. Then add a float number to it several times so that the variable's final data has a value greater than zero. Finally print out the number.

Sample code:

```
my_float = 0
#Add to the value of 'my_float' several times
print(my_float)
```

If your variable didn't add up you probably chose the wrong operator.

Exercise #3 - Comparing Numbers

In this exercise, you will compare variables. Each variable has an integer. Use the *print()* function along with an *f-string* to compare those variables. Here's an example:

```
#Create variables for my_number and mysterious_number!

print(f"Your number is greater than the mysterious
number? {my_number > mysterious_number}")

#Sample Output

Your number is greater than the mysterious number? False
```

Chapter 3

User Input, Strings, Lists, and Some Other Things

You will also learn String Methods, Tuples, Sets, Dictionaries, and Indexing

User Input

It's time to make your code actually customizable! Customizable means that you can make choices while the code is running. This customization is called user input. It gives Python the ability to ask the user for information. When the code uses user input, the program pauses until the user has entered some data. This makes the program interactive and more useful but at the same time makes the code more complex.

Now, how do you use user input, you may ask. Use the **input**() function. But it's not just that easy. You use the *input()* function together with a variable. This way the data that the user has entered will be assigned to the variable. Here's an example:

```
answer = input("What is your favorite food?   ")
```

One important thing to know about the *input()* function is that it will always give a string type of data. You can test this by typing the following:

```
answer = input("What is your favorite food?   ")
print(type(answer))
```

Did you get <class 'str'>? Yes! If you remember back from chapter 1, *str* means string. You will learn how to convert a data type in a later chapter.

Another good practice is to add a space after the text that you used as parameter. In the following sample input code:

```
name = input("What is your name?   ")
```

You can see that there is a space between the question mark and the ending quotation mark ("). So that when you type your input, it shows up one space away from the string.

Playing with user input, you can customize some variables for something cool! If you want to impress your friends, you can make the computer program say things about you. First, create some variables that will hold data about you. Here is an example:

```python
name = input("Your name:    ")
age = input("Your age:    ")
height = input("Your height:    ")
hobby = input("What you like to do:    ")
```

Then create a paragraph that describes you using the variables you just created and assign it to another variable.

```python
about_me = f"""
Hi {name}
who is {age} years old,
{height} tall,
and likes to {hobby}.
"""
```

Now print that variable.

```python
print(about_me)
```

What do you see? Yes, the computer knows you. Now go blow up your friends' minds.

String Methods and Dot Notation

Do you want to work more on strings? Because there is just the thing for you----string methods! These methods are useful for things like checking something in the string or changing a character within the string.

All but one of these string methods use the dot character (.) Yes it is a dot, or period, and it is essential to syntax as it is the connection to a variable in order to use the string method. This is called dot notation.

But before you learn more about that, learn the one function that doesn't need a dot notation --- the *len()* function.

len()

The *len()* function measures the length of a string (*len* is short for length). In other words, it counts the number of characters in the string and gives back the total. Here is how you use it:

```
name = "Alexander Graham Bell"
print(len(name))
```

The result should be 21.

But why is it 21? You counted 19 letters. Well, good that you asked. In Python the space is counted as a character.

The len() function is useful in checking the length of a data type.

The next string methods to learn are **upper()**, **lower()**, and **capitalize()**. They use the dot notation so they are connected to a variable using a dot (or period). For example using the previous variable *'name'* the code looks like this:

```
print(name.upper())
```

But why use dot notation rather than a function? In Python, dot notation helps with making code legible and somewhat similar to the English language structure. It organizes code to show the relation of each block of code. You will be using more dot notation when you become a more advanced coder.

upper()

If the string method **upper()** is connected with a dot to the previous variable *'name'*, it will return the uppercase version of the string which is "ALEXANDER GRAHAM BELL".

```
print(name.upper())
ALEXANDER GRAHAM BELL
```

lower()

The **lower()** method is just the opposite of the **upper()** method. If you connect it to the previous variable *'name'* you will get the lowercase version "alexander graham bell".

```
print(name.lower())
alexander graham bell
```

capitalize()

Now, the **capitalize()** string method. It will capitalize the first letter of the first word of the string. Take note that it only affects the first word as it will not capitalize any other words in the string.

```
name = "alexander graham bell"
print(name.capitalize())
Alexander graham bell
```

Cool, right? Now quickly, here is the rest of the string methods:

find()

It will find the index number of a certain letter within a string (you will learn what an index is soon). This string method requires a parameter. This parameter is the letter that you want to find in the string.

```
name = "Rene Descartes"
print(name.find('a'))
9
```

isdigit()

Returns a boolean True if the string is a digit.

```
name = "2354234"
print(name.isdigit())
True
```

isalpha()

Returns a boolean True if the string is a series of letters. A space is not counted as a letter and the method will return False.

```
name = "Dichlorodifluoromethane"
print(name.isalpha())
True
```

count()

Counts the number of characters in a string and returns that number.

```
greeting = "Hello wonderful world"
print(greeting.count())
21
```

replace()

Replaces a letter in a string. This string method requires two parameters. It will replace all the letters in the string defined by the first parameter with the letter defined by the second parameter.

```
greeting = "Hello wonderful world"
print(greeting.replace('o','X'))
HellX wXnderful wXrld
```

String Methods with User Input

Using string methods with user input is a good style to keep the code clean. It's also why dot notation is great and it will become important when you become a more skillful programmer.

Instead of coding this way:

```
user = input("Type your name: ")
print(user.upper())
```

You can use dot notation on the *input()* function and your code will look like this:

```
user = input("Type your name: ").upper()
print(user)
```

Strings methods are useful. Dot notation is important.

Lists (or Arrays)

A quick note about arrays before you read any further. Python unfortunately does not have built-in support for arrays. Python instead uses lists. If you like to use arrays in Python you can research the Python NumPy library.

Let's say you have three types of cars: a Ford, a Chevy, and a BMW. So, then you create three variables to hold these items.

```python
my_car1 = 'Ford'
my_car2 = 'Chevy'
my_car3 = 'BMW'
```

But doing it that way is a bit of a hassle and time consuming, especially since they are all cars. So the smart solution is to use an array! An array can store multiple values in one variable.

However, since Python does not support arrays, you use lists instead. List is one of four data types that store collections of data. The other three types are **Tuples**, **Sets**, and **Dictionaries**, which are all used differently.

A list is signified with square brackets **[ ]**. Elements are listed between the square brackets and separated by commas. If you use a list to store your above collection of cars, it will look like this:

```python
my_cars = ['Ford', 'Chevy', 'BMW']
```

Lists aren't limited to string data types only. A list can also store integers:

```python
birds = [5, 17, 4, 2, 2, 49]
```

And also booleans:

```python
quiz_answers = [True, True, False, True]
```

A list can also store different data types:

```python
info = ["John Apfelbaum", False, 234]
```

Here are some more information about lists:

List Elements Are Ordered

When you create a list, its elements are arranged in a defined order. If a new element is added to the list, it is stored at the end of the list. If you tried the following comparison code:

```
fruits_list1 = ['apple', 'orange', 'grape']
fruits_list2 = ['orange', 'apple', 'grape']
fruits_list1 == fruits_list2
```

Python will return False since the order of the lists are not equivalent. They have the same elements but arranged in different orders. Lists need to have the same elements in the same order to be equal.

Get ready, you are about to learn an important thing about lists!

Lists Are Indexed

When you use a list in a code you often need to access a single element from it. For this purpose lists are indexed. An index is a number that represents the position of an element within a list.

One very important thing to know about indices is that they always start at zero. Why zero? The computer reads the index of the first element as zero since it is zero spaces away from the start. It's that simple. The second index is one, the third index is two, and so on. Here is an illustration using our three-cars example:

Element	Ford	Chevy	BMW
Index	0	1	3

Now that you know the index of an element, you can access the element 'Chevy' pretty easily. You do this by first stating the list you want to access:

my_cars

Add an opening and closing square brackets:

my_cars[ ]

And inside the brackets you enter the index number you want to access:

my_cars[1]

Try the following code :

```
my_cars = ['Ford', 'Chevy', 'BMW']
print(my_cars[1])
```

If Python printed 'Chevy' then you did it correctly!

To repeat, first type the name of the list you want to use then add square brackets. Between the square brackets you enter the index nuber of the element you want to access. Python reads the list then gets the element as pointed to by the index. It then returns the element for further processing like print. Awesome, right?

To test your new knowledge, create another list of cars:

```
his_cars = ['Chevy','BMW','Ford','Honda']
```

Now compare elements from the two lists to see if they are equal. You can use the *double-equal* operator for this. Here is the code:

```
my_cars = ['Ford', 'Chevy', 'BMW']
his_cars = ['Chevy','BMW','Ford','Honda']
my_cars[2] == his_cars[0]
```

Try different index numbers and see if you can get a pattern of True and False outputs.

But wait! There are more to lists than just these features!

Lists Allow Duplicates

As you have learned earlier, lists are ordered and indexed. Since lists are indexed they also allow duplicates. This means duplicate elements can be stored in a single list.

For example this is a list with duplicates:

```
trees = ['Oak','Pine','Whitebark','Oak']
print(trees)
['Oak','Pine','Whitebark','Oak']
```

Cool! That's a lot of features but there are still more things you need to learn about lists!

List Slicing and Indexing

So far, you know that lists are ordered, indexed, and allow duplicates. What else can they do? Here's a scenario: what if you want to access two elements in a list? What about three elements? What about all elements after the first element? The answer is list slicing!

List Slicing

It is a method of selecting a range of elements from within a list. This is how you can access multiple elements or sections of a list. You can slice a list within a slice range. The slice range is defined by a starting index, a colon, and an ending index. The slice range replaces the single index number entered in the brackets.

To put this into action, create a new list that holds more objects:

```
bedroom_stuff = ['Bed','Desk','Computer','Lamp', 'Shelf','Chair','Books']
```

Access the list:

```
bedroom_stuff[ ]
```

And add a slice range, for example from the elements 'Desk' to 'Shelf':

```
bedroom_stuff[ 1 : 4 ]
```

Python will read the list and return the following elements:

```
['Desk', 'Computer', 'Lamp']
```

Here's what's happening: in the slice range the starting index is 1. The element in this position is 'Desk' and will be printed out. A colon sign is added to signify that it is a slice range. An ending index marks the end of the range.

But wait, why isn't the index 4 element 'Shelf' not included? The answer is that Python knows that the ending index is 4 but will not print the element. That is why the last element printed is 'Lamp' (it has an index of 3) and not the 'Shelf'.

Say you want to slice the list *'bedroom_stuff'* from 'Bed' to 'Chair'. So you slice the list like this:

```
bedroom_stuff[ 0:5 ]
```

Python will read the list and return the following elements:

```
['Bed','Desk','Computer','Lamp','Shelf']
```

But instead of writing bedroom_stuff[0:5] you can leave the zero out and write **bedroom_stuff[:5]** instead. Python will automatically know that the starting index is zero.

This technique is the same if you write bedroom_stuff[2:]. Python knows that the ending index is the last element in the list. See following example:

```
bedroom_stuff[2:]
['Computer','Lamp','Shelf','Chair','Books']
```

Skip Index

Let's reuse the *'bedroom_stuff'* list for a different scenario. What if you want to slice the list but skip every other element? You use a skip index to select the needed elements. So for example your defined list and needed elements are the following:

Defined List

```
['Bed','Desk','Computer','Lamp','Shelf','Chair','Books']
```

Needed Elements

```
['Bed', 'Computer', 'Shelf']
```

You can do this by adding a second colon and a skip index in the brackets. The skip index determines how many elements will be skipped. The following is a visual example:

Now if you want to slice the entire *bedroom_stuff* list, you can write this:

```
bedroom_stuff[0:7:2]
```

Or using the coding style that I prefer:

```
bedroom_stuff[::2]
```

Python will read the list and return the following elements:

```
['Bed','Computer','Shelf', 'Books']
```

Negative Index

Lists can also have negative indices. Similar to list slicing, negative index slicing (or negative indexing) is done by using negative numbers for the starting, ending, or skip index. In this case Python reads the index in reverse order. Confused a bit? Why not try it out!

```
bedroom_stuff[-2:]
```

Did you get this?

```
['Chair','Books']
```

It may seem a bit confusing, but the index was counted starting from the last element (or end of the list). To get a better idea, try this:

```
bedroom_stuff[:-3:-1]
```

Python should return the following elements:

```
['Books','Chair']
```

Yay! Now it is in reverse order! Here's what's happening: the starting index is blank so Python starts reading from the beginning (or end) of the list. The ending index (-3) is negative so Python will count the index in reverse starting from the end of the list.

What really makes the output come out in reverse order is the negative skip index (-1). If you wanted to print the entire list in reverse order, just get rid of the ending index. For example:

```
bedroom_stuff[::-1]
['Books','Chair','Shelf','Lamp','Computer','Desk','Bed']
```

Pretty cool, huh? Slicing or editing the index is very useful for lists and also for strings. How can they be used for strings? Well, strings have an index that is why you can use the *len()* function on a string. Each character is in an indexed position in the string so you can technically slice or reverse a string.

Changing Lists and List Methods

Here you are, learning the final features of lists that are taught in this book.

Lists are mutable, which means they're changeable! You can change them using methods made for lists. But before you use these methods, you can try using a simple operator ---- *addition assignment operator*. If you remember from the last chapter that operator is plus-equal **+=**

For example if you want to add the item 'Blanket' to the list *bedroom_stuff* , set that list up:

```
bedroom_stuff +=
```

Since you are adding an element to a list, use square brackets:

```
bedroom_stuff += ['Blanket']
```

Now if you type print(bedroom_stuff) you will see 'Blanket' in the list. Hooray! What you did just now is a mutation, or change, to the list. This technique will be very useful for adding items to a list.

del

Another way to mutate the list is using *del* ---- short for delete. This will remove an item from a list using the index. In other words we can use a slice range to delete an element from a list. This is what it looks like:

```
del bedroom_stuff[2]
```

This will delete the item at index 2. Now, use a slice range to clear out the list but keep the last element:

```
del bedroom_stuff[-2::-1]
print(bedroom_stuff)
['Blanket']
```

The use of **del** for removing elements is different from the method **remove**() which you will soon learn.

List Methods

Now onto the list methods. These methods use the dot notation so a method is connected to a list using a dot (or period) . The ones you'll learn in this book are **append(), remove(), insert(), pop(), clear()**, and **reverse()**.

Before you start changing the *bedroom_stuff* list, just reset it.

bedroom_stuff = ['Bed','Desk','Computer','Lamp', 'Shelf','Chair','Books']

Now you are ready!

append()

This method will append, or add, a new element to the end of a list. Its function is similar to the *addition assignment* operator. For example:

```
bedroom_stuff.append('Blanket')
print(bedroom_stuff)
[ 'Bed', 'Desk', 'Computer', 'Lamp', 'Shelf', 'Chair', 'Books', 'Blanket' ]
```

remove()

This method will remove a specified element. You need to use the name of the element you want to remove. For example remove the lamp:

```
bedroom_stuff.remove('Lamp')
print(bedroom_stuff)
[ 'Bed', 'Desk', 'Computer', 'Shelf', 'Chair', 'Books', 'Blanket' ]
```

insert()

This method will add an item at a specified index. You need two parameters for this method to work --- the index and the item. This is what it looks like:

```python
bedroom_stuff.insert(3, 'Painting')
print(bedroom_stuff)
['Bed', 'Desk', 'Computer', 'Painting', 'Shelf', 'Chair', 'Books', 'Blanket']
```

pop()

This method will remove an element at a specified index. You only need the index number as a parameter. This is what it looks like:

```python
bedroom_stuff.pop(2)
print(bedroom_stuff)
['Bed', 'Desk', 'Painting', 'Shelf', 'Chair', 'Books', 'Blanket' ]
```

clear()

This method will clear out a list aka remove every element. This is what it looks like:

```python
fruits=['apple', 'orange', 'banana', 'grape', 'peach']
fruits.clear()
print(fruits)
[]
```

reverse()

This method will reverse the order of a list. This is what it looks like:

```python
bedroom_stuff.reverse()
print(bedroom_stuff)
['Blanket', 'Books', 'Chair', 'Shelf', 'Painting', 'Desk', 'Bed']
```

Changing Lists Using Indices and Slice Ranges

This is it! The final way to change or mutate a list (as taught in this book)! We can add elements to a list using slice ranges.

Use the *bedroom_stuff* list for the following example ---- add a new element 'Pillow' in the list:

```
bedroom_stuff[1:1] = ['Pillow']
print(bedroom_stuff)
['Blanket', 'Pillow', 'Books', 'Chair', 'Shelf', 'Painting', 'Desk', 'Bed']
```

Now, why was a slice range used? Can't you use a simple index? Well you can change the list using a simple index but it will replace the element instead of adding a new element. For example:

```
bedroom_stuff[4] = 'Bin'
print(bedroom_stuff)
['Blanket', 'Pillow', 'Books', 'Chair', 'Bin', 'Painting', 'Desk', 'Bed']
```

What happened in that example? Instead of adding the element 'Bin' to the index 4, it replaced the item 'Shelf' with 'Bin'. The item 'Shelf' is gone. It's not what you intended to do. However, using an index to replace an element may become useful in some coding solutions.

Membership Operators

A common thing done with lists is checking if a certain element (or item) is in a list or not. You can do this operation using membership operators ---- the **in** and **not in**. These operators return either True or False depending on which operator you use and what item you're looking for.

in operator

If you want to check if an item is in a list, use the **in** operator. For example check if the item 'Lamp' is in the *bedroom_stuff* list:

```
'Lamp' in bedroom_stuff
False
```

The item 'Lamp' is not found in the list because you have removed it in a previous example ---- the code returns False.

not in operator

Now if you want to check if an item is not in a list, use the **not in** operator. For example check if the item 'Clothes' is not in the list:

```
'Clothes' not in  bedroom_stuff
True
```

The membership operators *in* and *not in* will be used often to make decisions and will be useful for coding exercises in later chapters. Within this topic, you have learned the **not** operator which can be used in other boolean statements.

Tuples

Yay! Now it's time to learn about Tuples (have fun pronouncing it). But don't worry about having to read a lot of text again!

A Tuple is also a data type that can store collections of data similar to lists. The difference between Tuples and Lists are seen in some of their features. Tuples are ordered, accessible through an index, and allow duplicates just like a list.

Tuples use Parentheses

Tuples are written using parentheses to store data instead of square brackets. This is how a tuple is created: For example create a tuple named rgb_colors and assign the red, green, and blue data into it.

```
rgb_colors = ('red', 'green', 'blue')
```

But parentheses aren't Tuple's major difference from a list. Its major difference is...

Tuples are Unchangeable

The major difference between tuples and lists is that tuples are unchangeable or immutable. This means we cannot add or remove any elements in a tuple. Once the tuple has been created, it cannot change.

Updating Tuples

Now you may wonder, "Updating Tuples? You just told me they're immutable!" Well, yes I did say it. But there is a way to work around this.

To change a tuple, you need to convert it to a list! After a tuple is converted to a list, you are able to use list methods to mutate it. Then you convert it back to a tuple. It is a roundabout trick --- but it works.

list() and tuple() constructors

To do the conversions, use the *list()* and *tuple()* constructors. This is what you need to convert a list to tuple (or vice versa). For example, convert the tuple *rgb_colors* to a list.

```
mylist = list(rgb_colors)
```

Now add an element to the list using the *append()* method:

```
mylist.append('orange')
```

Then convert the list to a tuple, assign it back to *rgb_colors*, then print it!

```
rgb_colors = tuple(mylist)
print(rgb_colors)
('red', 'green', 'blue', 'orange')
```

Combining Tuples

There is another way of adding an element to a tuple --- by combining a tuple with another tuple! For example this is the first tuple:

```
rgb_colors = ('red', 'green', 'blue')
```

Now create another tuple containing a single element. Write a comma after the element to make sure Python knows it is a tuple and not a string.

```
newcolor = ('orange',)
```

Then combine the two tuples using the *addition-assignment* operator. Finally, print it to see the contents of the updated tuple.

```
rgb_colors += newcolor
print(rgb_colors)
('red', 'green', 'blue', 'orange')
```

- However, you can only add elements to existing tuples using the combination method.
- The best way to mutate a tuple is to convert it first into a list.

When is a Tuple useful?

Very good question. You use tuples over lists when you don't want the stored collection of data to be changed. For example RGB color codes are perfect data for storing in a tuple. This collection of data should never be changed.

Sets

Just like lists and tuples, a set is a data type that can store collections of data in a single variable. A set differs from a list (and tuple) in its features. These features make a set unique and useful for coding solutions.

Before getting into the features of a set, you should know what a set looks like. Sets are written with curly brackets **{ }** to store data. The following is an example of a set:

```
mySet = {'apple','orange','banana','grape'}
```

If you print the set:

```
print(mySet)
```

You might see that the elements are printed out of order. Why is that? Because...

Sets Are Unordered

Sets are not ordered. You can print them out as many times as you like and each element will appear in a different position in the set.

```
print(mySet)
{'banana', 'grape', 'orange', 'apple'}

print(mySet)
{'orange', 'banana', 'apple', 'grape'}
```

Set Elements Cannot Be Accessed

Sets are unordered, you know that already. But that also means they are not indexed. You cannot use an index to access the set, slice the set, or even use an element's name to print out an element.

Give it a try anyway:

```
print(mySet[1])
Type Error

print(mySet[2:3])
Type Error

print(mySet['orange'])
Type Error
```

But what we can do is use the **in** membership operator to check if an item is present in the set. This is an example:

```
print('orange' in mySet)
True
```

We can also loop through the set and print out the elements but that's for another chapter where you learn about loops.

Sets Don't Allow Duplicates

A set doesn't allow duplicates. It cannot contain two of the same elements. If duplicates are assigned to a set, only one of the duplicates will be stored. Here's an example:

```python
mySet ={'apple','apple','orange','banana','guava'}
print(mySet)
{'banana','orange','guava','apple'}
```

Set Methods

Sets are changeable but you can only mutate them using methods. Similar to lists, sets have methods to add and remove elements.

add()

This method will add an element to the set. Here's an example:

```python
mySet.add('grape')
print(mySet)
{'banana','orange','guava','apple','grape'}
```

remove()

This method will remove an element from the set. Here's an example:

```python
mySet.remove('orange')
print(mySet)
{'banana','guava','apple','grape'}
```

discard()

This method will discard an element from the set. Here's an example:

```python
mySet.discard('guava')
print(mySet)
{'banana','apple','grape'}
```

The difference between the *discard()* and *remove()* methods is that *remove()* will output an error message if the element is not found in the set while *discard()* does not.

clear()

This method will remove all elements from the set. Here's an example:

```
mySet.clear()
print(mySet)
{}
```

Lists, Tuples, and Sets all store collections of data but differ from each other in many ways. Now it's time to learn about an incredible way to pair data with other data using dictionaries.

Dictionaries

Yay! Something that you've already heard of --- dictionaries! It may not sound as interesting but they are powerful!

Note: Lets go over how to create a dictionary, how to access it, and in exercises or challenges you will learn how to mutate it.

A dictionary stores multiple values in **key:value** pairs. This means for every **key** there is a **value** attached to it. It is similar to a real dictionary where words are paired with definitions.

The following is an example of a dictionary:

```
my_car = {
         'Brand': "Ford",
         'Model': "Mustang",
         'Year': "1964"
       }
```

Why is it spaced out like that? Because it is much easier to see and read the *key:value* pairs. It will still work if you do it another way:

```
my_car = { 'Brand': "Ford", 'Model': "Mustang", 'Year': "1964" }
```

Obviously, this style of writing gets long and confusing very quickly.

Now it's time to explain how to make a dictionary.

A dictionary uses curly brackets **{ }** to store data in *key:value* pairs. Looking at the above dictionary *my_car,* you will see that the first key is 'Brand'. You can refer to this key to access the value it is paired with, which in this case is "Ford".

To create these pairs, write a colon between the key and value. The colon will pair them up. After that, the pair is considered a single element, so you add a comma after.

As stated earlier, you can access a dictionary by referring to a key. The key must be inside square brackets. Here's how you can make the code search for 'Brand' in the dictionary *my_car* and return the value it is paired with.

```
print(my_car['Brand'])
Ford
```

More examples:

```
print(my_car['Model'])
Mustang
print(my_car['Year'])
1964
```

Awesome, right? These dictionaries will be very useful in coding when the time comes and you will learn how to change dictionaries later on.

Wow, this chapter was pretty long. That's how important these topics are! You have currently learned the basics about the four data types that can store multiple values in one variable. You've also learned string methods and user input.

Very soon you might be able to create a basic text game! But to run a game, the program needs to be able to make decisions! That's what you are going to learn in the next chapter ---- decision making!

Good job! You've learned a lot! Be proud of yourself!

Chapter 3 Quick Review

User Input:
• User Input gives the code the ability to ask the user for data input.
• User Input pauses the code from running until an input has been entered.
• You can use variables with user input and use them in *F-Strings*.

String Methods and Dot Notation:
• String Methods are used to check or change strings.
• The string method *len()* returns the length of a string variable.
• Other string methods use dot notation.
• Dot notation organizes the code.

Lists:
• Lists are one of four data types that can store collections of data, meaning they can hold multiple values in one variable.
• Lists can store strings, integers, booleans and other data types.
• Lists use square brackets [ ] to store data.
• Lists are ordered, indexed, can be mutated, and allow duplicates.
• You can use the addition assignment operator, *del*, or string methods to mutate lists.

List Slicing and Indexing:
• List slicing is a method of selecting a range of elements in a list.
• Use list slicing to access multiple elements at once.
• Slice ranges are used for slicing and consist of a starting index, a colon, and an ending index.
• A skip index can be added to a slice range which will skip a number of indices.
• Negative indexing is where the indices in a range are negative and indexing starts at the end of the list.

Membership Operators:
- check if an object is in a list or not.
- returns either True or False.
- are *in* and *not in*.
- are useful for making decisions.

Tuples:
- are data types that can store collections of data.
- use parentheses ( ) .
- are unchangeable, so values cannot be changed.
- allow duplicates.
- can be changed by using the *list()* and *tuple()* constructors.
- are used to store data that shouldn't be changed, like RGB colors.

Sets:
- are data types that can store collections of data.
- use curly brackets { } .
- are changeable.
- are unordered. This means they are not indexed either.
- cannot be accessed with a key or index.
- don't allow duplicates.
- Elements can be added to and removed from sets using set methods.

Dictionaries:
- store multiple values in key:value pairs.
- For every key element, there is a value attached to it.
- use curly brackets { } .
- can be accessed by referring to a key. The code will return the value of the key.
- are usually written in indented format.

In the next chapter, you will learn how to code decision-making using **if - else** conditional statements.

Chapter 3 Exercises

Exercise #1 - **Mad Libs 2.0**

In this exercise, you will create another version of Mad Libs! This time, each variable will use the *input()* function! Here's a sample output:

> #The variables used are 'animal', 'name', 'adjective', and 'food'
>
> # sample output
>
> There once lived a sheep named Wallie. Wallie is very handsome because he eats apple.

Exercise #2 - **Test time!**

In this exercise, you will create a test! The test questions are based on True or False. After the questions, the program should print the results for your test.

Use a *list* that contains the correct answers for the test.
Use *input()* in variables to ask the questions.

Here is an example of results from a test:

> True or False: An apple is an orange? true
> True or False: Do you like cake? false
> True or False: The author is cool? false
>
> Your results:
>
> Question One | Your Answer: true - Correct Answer: False
> Question Two | Your Answer: false - Correct Answer: True
> Question Three | Your Answer: false - Correct Answer: True

Exercise #3 - **The Length of a Secret Message**

For this exercise, you need to create a program that will ask the user to type a message and print the length of that message. Here's some code that you can use:

```
secret_message = # Fill in the missing code!
message_length = # Fill in the missing code!
print(# You could use an f-string!)
```

Exercise #4 - **Comparing Test Answers**

For this exercise, reuse the code from exercise 3. Instead of printing the results of the answers, compare the user's answers to the correct answers.

Declare a variable that has an empty list.

After every question, add the answer to the list.

After all the questions have been asked, compare the user's answers to the correct answers to see if they match.

Hint: Instead of using Booleans for the correct answers, use strings.

Example: 'False' or 'True'.

Here's a sample output:

```
True or False: An apple is an orange?  False
True or False: Do you like cake?  True
True or False: The author is cool?  True
Is the entire test correct? True
```

Exercise #5 - **Fruit Guesser**

In this exercise, you will write a program that asks the user to name a fruit. Then check if the answer is in a set of fruits.

Use a membership operator to check.

Here's an example of some code and output:

```
fruits = ('apple', 'banana', 'pear', 'grapes', 'peach')
guess = #Write code here!
print(f"Is it a real fruit? #Fill this in!")
Name a fruit:  apple
Is it a real fruit? True
```

Chapter 4

if-else Statements

You will also learn if-elif-else, conditions, and indentation

Decisions and Decision-making

You make decisions every single day, every hour, and every minute. If you were to map out these decisions on a flow chart, it would look something like this:

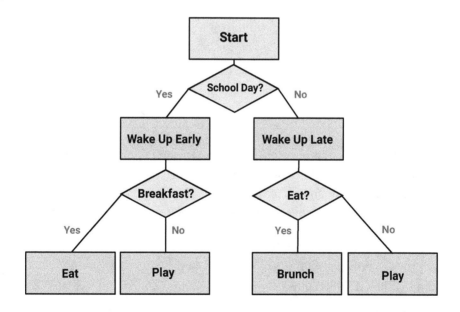

Now this is a simple chart of the idea of decisions. For every question you encounter, you either answer yes or no to it. The idea of answering yes or no is just like True or False conditions, or in other word –booleans. Since it is using booleans, it often has a condition.

Okey, first imagine how your day would go. Think it is a Monday morning, the dreaded Monday morning, because it is time for school. Should you wake up early or late? Since it is a school day, you wake up early. But you can also decide to sleep in. These are situations that require you to make decisions.

Now what should you eat for breakfast? Something healthy or a quick snack? If you slept in, you would need to eat quickly so you can get to school on time. But if you woke up early, you could have a nice breakfast. This is another set of situations that need decision-making.

Now, skip to school, should you be organized? Should you listen to the teacher? Should you bring your textbook? Should you do this? Do that? It can go on and on and on. From all these questions you need to make decisions, and you either say yes or no to these questions.

Condition

A condition is a requirement that must be met in order for an action to be done. If you look back to the above flow chart, you can see the condition in order for an outcome to play out. If it is True that it is a school day, you wake up early. If it is False that it is a school day, you wake up late. Let's visualize this:

> School day = True
> Is it a school day?
> If True, Wake Up Early
> If False, Wake Up Late

The condition you see here is *if it is a school day*. If it is, you wake up early. If not, you wake up late. One word that you notice coming up many times is **if** .

if Statement

if statements are used in code to make decisions. These statements work with comparison and logical operators, checking if the condition is met ---- meaning True. When the *if statement* is True, any indented code following the statement will be run.

The following is an example of an *if statement*:

```
school_day = True
if school_day is True:
    print("Wake up! It's a school day!")
```

Here's what's happening in the above example: You have a variable named *school_day* which holds a boolean value ---- in this example it is set to True . Following it is an *if statement* which is constructed like this:

Here's a generic way of looking at it:

if **variable** operator **condition:**

Looking at how this *if statement* is constructed, you see it starts with an *if* and ends with a colon : An *if* obviously signals Python that it is an *if statement*. The colon is used to complete the statement and to indent the lines of code that follow it.

Why do you need to indent the lines of code? This is to group the code that follows the *if statement* into a single block of code that will be run if the condition in the statement is True.

If the condition is not met ---- meaning False, Python will skip over the indented lines of code ---- meaning it will not be run.

The following is an example of indented lines of code:

```
if variable is True:
    print("This variable is true!")
    print("Wow!")
    print("Indented code!")
```

Now, you don't necessarily need to use **is** or **true** in *if statements*. You can cut it down to:

```
if school_day:
    print("Wake up! It's a school day!")
```

By default, the *if statement* already checks if the variable is True.

But if you want check if it is False, then you add the **not** operator:

```
if not school_day:
    print("No school today! Sleep yo!")
```

Alright, that's cool! But why can you only use variables and booleans? Well, first off, you're wrong. You can use other data types like integers, lists, strings, etc. Here's an example:

```
my_list = ['apple', 'oreo', 'chicken']
an_item = 'apple'
if an_item in my_list:
    print(f"{an_item} in list")
```

Also, comparison operators are commonly used with *if statements*. For example:

```
a = 10+15
b = 25
if a == b:
    print(f"{a} is equal to {b}")
```

Here's one example with strings:

```
mytext = "This is a string!"
if mytext == "This is a string!":
        print(True)
```

Now you might think the examples are different each time and you'd need to learn different types of *if statements*, but no!

Looking back at how an *if statement* is constructed, you see that every element of the statement is present in the examples.

Let's look at this *if statement*:

```
if a == b:
        print(True)
```

The variable here is **a** (and b), the operator is **==** and the condition is the default True. So, this *if statement* is checking:

> *If the statement "variable 'a' is equal to variable 'b' " is True, then print the boolean 'True'.*

To sum up what you just learned:

> **if statements** have conditions that must be met for the following lines of code to be run.

> **if statements** can use different types of variables like integer, boolean, and other data types.

Get it now? I'm sure you do!

The *if statements* are very important. So don't forget them!

if, else Statements

There comes a time when the *if statement* condition is not met and any indented line of code is skipped ---- not run. Now, of course, you don't want these lines of code to be run because the condition is not met.

But what if you want to run alternate lines of code if the condition is not met? Well, you might think you would just not indent lines of code in the first place, like for example:

```
y = 5
if y > 10:
        print("IT IS GREATER")
print("IT IS LESS")
```

not indented

The output is:

```
IT IS LESS
```

The above example worked since 5 is not greater than 10 --- the condition is False, so the indented first *print()* function is skipped and instead the non-indented second *print()* function is executed.

But if you change the value of the variable:

```
y = 15
if y > 10:
        print("IT IS GREATER")
print("IT IS LESS")
```

The output is:

```
IT IS GREATER
IT IS LESS
```

Oh no! You've just printed out both strings!
You only wanted to print "IT IS GREATER".

You can fix this by adding   an **else statement**. An *else statement* concludes an *if statement* if the condition is not met ---- is not True. This means that if the condition is true, Python will run   the line of code following the *if statement*. Otherwise, the code under the *else statement* will run.

This is what a proper *if, else statement* looks like:

```
y = 15
if y > 10:
        print("IT IS GREATER")
else:
        print("IT IS LESS")
```

The *else statement* does not contain anything besides the word **else** followed by a colon. This is because it is simply the alternate action of an *if statement*. Any indented code following the *else statement* will run if the condition is False.

Now, what if you want to have multiple *if, else* statements? You would need to add an *if* and *else* statements under the original *else statement* and so on and so forth. It could become very hard to read. A better way is to use an **elif** statement.

if, elif, and else

elif is basically the combination of else and if. You use *elif* to add another condition if the first *if statement* is False.

```
y = 15
if y > 10:
        print("IT IS GREATER")
elif y < 10:
        print("IT IS LESS")
else:
        print("IT IS PROBABLY EQUAL")
```

elif cannot be used before an *if statement* or after an *else statement*.

Now why can't you just use another if statement? Well, if you did, this is what it would look like if you didn't use *elif*. It can become very hard to follow.

```
if condition:
        print("CLEAR 1")
else:
        if condition:
                print("CLEAR 2")
        else:
                if condition:
                        print("CLEAR 3")
                else:
                        print("END")
```

else and *if* were combined to form *elif* to make the code look cleaner and easier to read. For example:

```
if condition:
        print("CLEAR 1")
elif condition:
        print("CLEAR 2")
elif condition:
        print("CLEAR 3")
else:
        print("END")
```

Now you know how to use *if, elif* and *else*! You can use them to make different decisions in your code.

But what if you want to have multiple conditions in ONE *if statement*? What if you want to have AT LEAST ONE condition to be true? Find out soon on the Coding Show at 7 o'clock tonight! (That was a joke.)

Seriously now, the answers will be revealed in the following topics. So read on!

if Statements with Logical and Membership Operators

Remember the logical and membership operators from a couple chapters back? The logical operators are **and, or,** and **not**. The membership operators are **in** and **not in**. You can use these operators in *if statements*. Let's start off with logical operators.

When you use logical operators in *if statements*, they aren't always in a specific position. For example:

```python
if (x and y) or not z:
    print(True)
```

Now this is a bit complicated since all the logical operators and parentheses are used, but what you should learn from this is that logical operators can be in different positions. The above example can be rewritten this way and still works the same:

```python
if not z or (y and x):
    print(True)
```

Now, of course, they can't just go randomly anywhere in the expression, but logical operators go around data types and sometimes next to other operators.

and operator

Imagine you have two button switches. These two switches connect to a lightbulb. If you press one button, the lightbulb doesn't light up. If you press the other, the lightbulb still isn't on. But if you press both buttons at the same time the lightbulb turns on.

You can see an illustration on the next page.

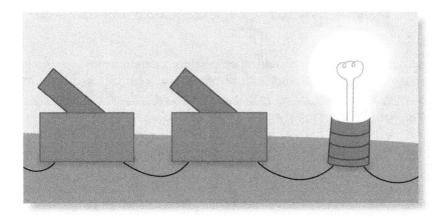

This idea of two buttons can easily be translated to two conditions. The lightbulb translates to the indented code. When you press a button, this button is in a True state. When it's not pressed, it's in a False state.

The idea of the lightbulb and buttons will be used to explain the other logical operators.

By now you got the idea. Both conditions (two conditions in one boolean expression) need to be true if you want Python to run the indented code. You can add two conditions to an *if statement* by using the **and** operator. This operator simply combines two of the same data types in a boolean expression. Here is an example:

```
if x and y:
    #any code here
```

The conditions x and y both need to be true for the code to run. You can also add a third condition by adding another **and** operator:

```
if x and y and z:
    #any code here
```

or operator

Imagine the two buttons and lightbulb again. Instead of having both buttons needed to turn on the lightbulb, only one is needed. Either button will work to turn on the lightbulb.

This expression is possible by using an **or** operator. Just like how it's called, an *or* operator takes in two conditions and checks if either one is true. If so, it will return True. It will also return True if both conditions are true.

Here is an example:

```
if x or y:
        #any code here
```

Similar to the *and* operator, you can use this operator multiple times to add more conditions

For example:

```
if x or y or z:
        #any code here
```

not operator

The not operator simply reverses the state of a boolean condition. If the state is True, adding a **not** will make it False. On the opposite, if the state is False, adding a **not** will make it True.

The two operators you have learned (*and, or*) have been checking if the conditions are true. There will be a time when a condition needs to be False for the statement to be True.

If that sounds confusing, the following nice chart will make it easier to understand.

**Operator checks if
condition is
False**

**Condition is False,
this returns True**
(*Because the
statement is false and
is being checked if it is
False*)

**Returned state is True
so run code**

The *not* operator is the one checking if the condition is False. It is similar to the *not in* membership operator which also expects the condition to be false but made for lists. Both operators work in *if statements* but for now just focus on the *not* operator.

Here's another example:

```
x = False
if x is not True:
        print(False)
```

Here's the shortened version of the above example:

```
x = False
if not x:
        print(False)
```

Ok that's cool, but why is there a long and short version? Well, both of them translate to checking *if x is not True*. In the short version, the combination of *if* and *not* operators commands Python to check if x is not True.

Consider using the **not** operator multiple times in a single boolean expression. You might think it is easily used like the other two earlier operators but in reality it is very strange and can be perplexing.

Think of the *not* operator as a negative value. Computers follow math and in math two negatives make a positive. This means when you use two *not* operators like in the following example...

```
if not not x:
        #any code here
```

...you are checking for a positive (instead of a negative) and positive means True.

Try this one:

```
if not not not x:
        #any code here
```

Don't worry about having to use it though! If you understand the concept of negative and positive, no matter how many times the *not* operator is repeated, it will always switch from positive to negative to positive to negative and so on.

To conclude this topic, a *not* operator cannot check more than one condition alone. You will need to use other operators as well.

Complex Decisions using Logical Operators

You can use logical operators multiple times. Different types of logical operators can be used in one boolean expression.

Say for example you have three switch buttons and a lightbulb. The lightbulb is normally on. If you press at least one of the buttons, the lightbulb turns off. If you translate this to code language, you basically want all conditions to be False so that the indented code will be run. You can achieve this by using both the *and* operator and the *not* operator several times.

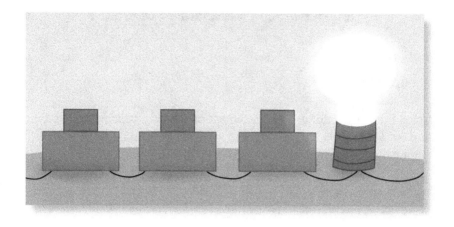

Here is the sample code:

```
if not x and not y and not z:
        print("Light bulb is on")
else:
        print("Light bulb is off")
```

Now, replace the last *and* operator and *not* operator with an *or* operator.

```
if not x and not y or z:
        print("Light bulb is on")
else:
        print("Light bulb is off")
```

The above code is checking if x and y are not True or if z is True. A better way to write this is by using parentheses to group the *and* conditions.

```
if (not x and not y) or z:
        print("Light bulb is on")
else:
        print("Light bulb is off")
```

Decisions using Membership Operators

in operator

Using the **in** operator in an *if statement* checks if a specific item is found in a variable of the type that stores a collection of data like *list*, *tuple*, or *dictionary*. For example a list:

```python
my_cars = ['Ford', 'Chevy', 'BMW']
if 'BMW' in my_cars:
    print("Yes! I got a BMW!")
```

Another example using a tuple:

```python
rgb_colors = ('red', 'green', 'blue')
if 'blue' in rgb_colors:
    print("Color blue is available!")
```

not in operator

The **not in** operator is the opposite of **in** operator. Use this in an *if statement* if you want to know that a specific item is not in the *list*, or *tuple*, or *dictionary*. For example you want to verify that 'Audi' is not in the list:

```python
my_cars = ['Ford', 'Chevy', 'BMW']
if 'Audi' not in my_cars:
    print("Oh no, got no Audi!")
```

CONGRATULATIONS!

Yay! You learned important coding knowledge in this chapter!

Chapter 4 Quick Review

If Statements

You learned:

- that *if statements* are used to make decisions in code.
- that *if statements* use different kinds of operators for conditions.
- that booleans work in *if statements*.
- how to write an *if statement*.
- *else statements*
- how *else statements* are used if the first if statement's condition is not met.
- *elif statements*
- how *elif statements* are used for another decision after the first *if statement*.

If Statements with Logical and Membership Operators

- You learned how to use logical and membership operators in if *statements*.
- You worked with *and, not*, and *or operators* in *if statements*.

Chapter 4 Exercises

Exercise #1 - **Password Lock**

In this exercise, you will create a password lock! The program will contain a "secret password" that the user must type to access a message.

Use an *if statement* to check if the user's input matches with the password. If so, print a message!

Here's a sample output:

> #First Run
> What is the password? password
> Sorry, that is not the correct password
> #Second Run
> What is the password? cookies
> Correct! You get free cookies!

Exercise #2 - **Story Game**

It's time to make a game! A story game to be exact. By using the power of *if statements* you can create a story game!

Use variables with the *input()* function to store the user's choices.
Use *if, elif,* or *else* statements to compare the user's choice to create different outcomes based on the user's choice.

Here's an example of a short story game:

> What is your name? Jason
> Welcome, Jason, to Story Game!
> A man in a dark cloak approaches you and asks you to
> follow him. Will you: [1]Follow or [2] Ignore
> # User chose 1
> __YOU FOLLOW THE MAN__
> The man offers you a shiny key.
> Will you: [1]Take it or [2]Decline his offer
> # User chose 1
> __YOU ACCEPT THE OFFER__
> The golden key suddenly teleports you into empty space.
> You'll probably die out there.
> THE END: You died!

Exercise #3 - Geoguessr

© Permission to print from Yzabella Latorilla

Have you ever heard of the game Geoguessr? It is a game where you are placed in a random location and you must guess your location. For this exercise, you are going to make a mini version of Geoguessr where the player is prompted with clues to his location. He must then try to guess the continent of his location.

To make your code smarter, use a list that holds the correct answers for each location. Use a variable to hold the total score. After every prompt, use an *if statement* to check the player's guess. If the guess is correct, add one point to the score.

Here's an example of an output:

> You are in the middle of nowhere.
> It's freezing and the environment you are in is full of snow and glaciers.
> There are penguins walking nearby.
> What continent are you on?
> YOUR GUESS: antarctica
>
> Your total score: 3 out of 3

Chapter 5

Type Casting and Loops

You will learn for and while loops, iteration, counter variable, conditions

Type Casting

Type casting converts data from one type to another — for example from string to integer or from float to string. It is done by using the functions *int()*, *float()*, and *str()*. These functions return values that were converted to the specific and desired data type.

int()

This function will construct an integer number from a float, or string, or another integer. For example:

```
a_float = 5.92
print(int(a_float))
5
```

Converting a float to an integer will remove all decimal numbers

Here's another example:

```
mystring = "239"
myint = int(mystring) + 100
print(myint)
339
```

float()

This function will construct a float from an integer, another float or a string. For example:

```
mystring = "4"
print(float(mystring))
4.0
```

str()

This function will construct a string from an integer, another string, or other data types. For example:

```
my_cars = ['Ford', 'Chevy', 'BMW']
print(str(my_cars))
['Ford', 'Chevy', 'BMW']
```

LOOPS

An important advantage of using computers is that they can repeat actions or calculations multiple times very fast. The way you can make a computer program repeat a code or parts of it multiple times is by using a loop statement. The two main loops in Python are the **for loop** and the **while loop**.

for loop

A *for loop* is a statement that is used to iterate over a code sequence. You use a *for loop* to repeat a block of code a specific number of times. Here is an example of a *for loop* statement:

```
nr_group = [1, 2, 3, 4, 5, 6, 7]
for number in nr_group:
        print(number)
```

The resulting output will be like this:

```
1
2
3
4
5
6
7
```

You may be confused but let's go over how a *for loop* is constructed and used.

Constructing a For Loop

A *for loop* consists of the **for** (start of the loop), the iterator (or indexing variable), the **in** (membership operator), and a group of items (which defines the number of times the loop is repeated), and the colon (end of the statement).

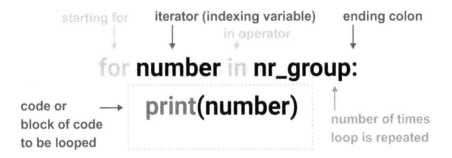

Iterating Through For Loops

You previously used a list to define the number of times of iteration. But that's not the only way to do it.

You can also iterate a specific number of times within a specific range of numbers. To do this, replace the iterator with a variable named "**i**" which is a standard variable name for iterators in Python, then replace the list with the **range()** function. The *range()* function can take in up to three parameters. But for now, use just one parameter to iterate a specific number of times.

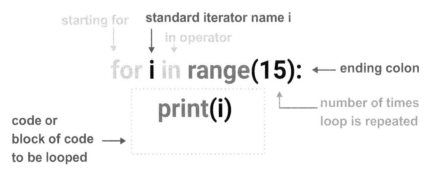

Using One Parameter (Basic Iteration)

range()

Let's say you want to print the word "Cookie" fifteen times. You create a variable that holds the string "Cookie" and use a *for loop* statement to iterate a *print()* function fifteen times.

The number 15 (as an integer) will be the parameter of the *range()* function. You can use the letter **i** as an iterator, but any name or letter that makes sense will work. Here's a sample code:

```
word = 'Cookie'
for i in range(15):
    print(word)
```

The output should be the word "Cookie" printed fifteen times!

Using Two Parameters (Range Iteration)

Great, you can use a specific number to iterate a code. But not only that, you can also iterate using a range of numbers. If you wanted to start at the number 20 and iterate until 50, you can do that by using two parameters. The first parameter will be the starting number and the second parameter will be the ending number. For example:

```
for i in range(20,50):
    print(i)
```

Using Three Parameters (Step Iteration)

Adding a third parameter gives the *range()* function a **step parameter**. Similar to the skip index used for lists, the step parameter will skip a specific number of items when iterating. If you wanted to print the multiples of 5 between 10 and 30, the *range()* function must have three parameters — 10, 30, and 5.

For example:

```
for i in range(10,30,5):
        print(i)
```

The output will be the multiples of 5 between 10 and 30.

```
10
15
20
25
```

while **loop**

The second type of loop is the **while loop**. It also repeats a block of code but what makes it different from *for loop* is that it uses a boolean expression. The *while loop* only repeats a block of code as long as the boolean expression remains true. While loops can also be interpreted as conditional loops, or in other words, loops that only iterate while a condition is true.

Here's an example:

```
mycounter = 0
while mycounter < 15:
        print(mycounter)
        mycounter += 1
```

In the above example the variable *mycounter* is the counter variable and was initially set to 0. The *while loop* has the condition that when *mycounter* is less than 15 the loop runs the block of code following it.

Incrementing a counter variable in a Loop

The *while loop* expression itself does not increment the value of *mycounter* therefore you have to add a line of code that increments the *mycounter*. This is done with *mycounter += 1* line. Once the *mycounter* reaches the value 15 (making condition False) the loop breaks.

Constructing a While Loop

A *while loop* starts with **while** followed by a conditional expression and a colon. Within the block of code that loops, add a line of code that eventually makes the conditional expression False to break the loop.

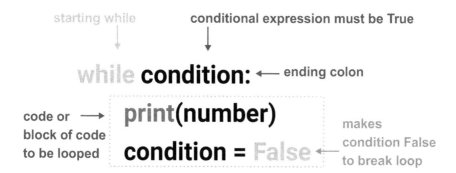

starting while   conditional expression must be True

while **condition:** ← ending colon

code or → **print(number)**   makes
block of code   condition False
to be looped **condition = False** ← to break loop

Here's another example, this time using the *input()* function to make the condition False and break the loop.

```
hidenumber = 20
guess = input("Guess a number: ")
while not int(guess) == hidenumber:
        print("Wrong guess!")
        guess = input("Your guess? ")
print("Correct guess!")
```

The condition in the above example is ' not int(guess) == hidenumber '. The line of code that could eventually make the condition False is ' **guess** = input("Your guess? ") '.

Once you entered the number 20 the *while loop* breaks and the code proceeds to print out "Correct guess!"

If the *while condition* never becomes False, the loop will get stuck in a non-ending cycle and the program could freeze.

Wow! You learned the loops!

Chapter 5 Quick Review

Type Casting

You learned:
- that type casting converts data from one type to another.
- that the type casting functions are *int()*, *float()*, and *str()*.
- how to use type casting.

Loops

You learned that:
- loops can repeat actions or calculations multiple times.
- there are two types of loops: *for loop* and *while loop*

For Loops

You learned:
- that a *for loop* is a statement used to iterate over a code sequence.
- that *for loops* repeat blocks of code a specific number of times.
- how to create a *for loop*.
- how to use the *range()* function in a *for loop*.
- the three types of iterating in a *for loop* using the *range()* function.

While Loops

You learned:
- that *while loops* use boolean expressions.
- that they can also be interpreted as conditional loops
- that they are loops that iterate only while the condition is true.
- how to use a counter variable along with incrementing, or adding.
- how to create a *while loop*.

Chapter 5 Exercises

Exercise #1 - **Converting Responses**

In this exercise, you will need to fix a piece of code. This code appears to have some wrong data types. Try fixing the code with only type casting. *Hint: There is more than one way to fix the code.*

```
score = 564
random_number = '564'
favorite_number = '28'

if score == random_number:
    print("Yay!")

if favorite_number == 28:
    print("Cool Number!")
```

Exercise #2 - **List of Traits**

In this exercise, you will need to print out a list of traits of a person. Here's an example:

```
person_traits = ['john doe', 'tall', 'science']
#Name: john doe
#height: tall
#major: science
```

Use a for loop to iterate through the list and print out each trait, BUT print them out in *f-strings*. How? Use *if statements* to check for each trait. Here's an example output:

```
My name is john doe
I am tall
My major is science
```

Exercise #3 - **Infinite Numbers**

For this exercise, write a program that uses a loop to print out numbers forever. You can do this in two ways:

FOR LOOP VERSION

Declare a variable with a large number. Use this variable as your parameter for the *range()* function.

Use two *for loops*, one within the other. In the second *for loop*, print out the iterator and increment the variable with another large number.

The problem with this is that it will eventually end at some point. But running it for a couple of minutes gives the impression that it goes on forever.

WHILE LOOP VERSION

Use a *while loop* statement where the condition never becomes true. Increment by a number after printing.

Exercise #4 - **Guess the Number!**

In this exercise, you will create a number guessing game! The game should ask the player to pick a number between a set range of numbers. If the player gets it wrong, the game will ask him again.

Use a *while loop* to make sure that the player's guess is not equal to the number.
Use *if, elif,* and *else statements* to check if the guess is correct, great than, less than, or not valid.

Here's an example output:

```
Pick a number between 0 and 20: #Player chose 3
That number is too low. Try again.

Pick a number between 0 and 20: #Player chose 13
Correct!
```

Chapter 6

Turtle Graphics - Your Pet Turtle

You will learn Turtle graphics, Module, RGB, Hexadecimal system

The Turtle Module

When you download Python, it comes with a lot of cool prewritten, ready-to-use code that you can use in your own coding projects - to solve real world problems or even just to play with. This prewritten code is called a **module**. A module is a Python file with blocks of code grouped together and can work with each other. In this chapter, you will be learning a graphic module called **turtle**.

To begin using the turtle graphic module, like any other module, you need to **import** it. Importing a module allows you to use that module in your own code.

For starters, type the keywords *import* and *turtle* (the name of the turtle graphic module) in the IDLE Shell or Editor.

```
import turtle
```

It looks like this in IDLE Shell:

```
● ● ●                    *IDLE Shell 3.10.0*
      Python 3.10.0 (v3.10.0:b494f5935c, Oct  4 2021, 14:59:
      20) [Clang 12.0.5 (clang-1205.0.22.11)] on darwin
      Type "help", "copyright", "credits" or "license()" for
      more information.
>>>
>>>  import turtle


                                             Ln: 4  Col: 13
```

Note: Nothing else should show up just yet.

Now you know how to import a module! All you need to do is write the *import* command and add the name of the module of your choice to make more impressive code!

At this point you are ready to use the *turtle* module!

Creating Your Pet Turtle

Right after importing the turtle module, nothing should happen. But it means you did it correctly! Right now Python has established access to the turtle module and is waiting for the proper commands from your code ---- this allows you to create a turtle!

shape()

To create a turtle, use a special function called **shape()**. Note that this function is pre-written inside the module, it doesn't show on your own code and you don't need to write it yourself. This function will tell Python what shape you want the turtle to have. It also uses the dot notation technique. Here's what the line of code should look like:

```
turtle.shape('turtle')
```

Go ahead and type that into the IDLE Shell. Click Enter and a new window will pop up with a turtle!

Two Windows

When you use the turtle module you will get two open windows —– the IDLE Shell window and the Python Turtle Graphics window where your turtle is displayed. The code you write in the IDLE Shell window controls what is being displayed in the graphics window.

The graphics screen with the turtle is composed of two objects, a **screen object** and a **turtle object**. The turtle module that created these objects contains prewritten functions that you can play around with to create some interesting graphics!

setup()

Before diving into the graphics part, one final setting should be set and it's the size of the window. By using the **setup()** function the window is adjusted to a specific size to make it easier to work with.

```
turtle.setup(500,500)
```

A Turtle In The Ocean (The Screen Object)

bgcolor()

Ok, so you have a cute little turtle chilling in a white window. Not really a good natural environment for a turtle, so go ahead and change that! You can change the window's background color by using the *screen object's* **bgcolor()** function. You can do that by writing the following line:

```
turtle.Screen().bgcolor('light green')
```

This may look confusing at first, but this is an ingenious way of formatting code in a modern programming style called **dot notation**. By using dots we connect objects with functions to show the relationship between them.

So here's what's happening in that line of code. First the screen object was connected to the turtle object. *Screen()* is an object that belongs to the turtle module.

```
turtle.Screen()
```

Then the *bgcolor()* function was connected to the screen object. It has the parameter 'light green' that tells the computer to change the background color to light green.

```
turtle.Screen().bgcolor('light green')
```

If you have followed everything correctly so far your IDLE Shell should look something like this:

```
IDLE Shell 3.10.0

Python 3.10.0 (v3.10.0:b494f5935c, Oct  4 2021, 14:59:
20) [Clang 12.0.5 (clang-1205.0.22.11)] on darwin
Type "help", "copyright", "credits" or "license()" for
 more information.
>>>
>>> import turtle
>>> turtle.shape('turtle')
>>> turtle.setup(500,500)
>>> turtle.Screen().bgcolor('light green')
>>>

                                    Ln: 5  Col: 22
```

And your turtle graphics window should look like this:

Wait, that background color doesn't fit the looks of a jungle. Although it is technically green, it is a light shade of green. Ok don't worry, there is a way to use different shades of green. Let's talk about how colors work on computer screen.

The Color Brothers: RGB and Hexadecimal

Computers cannot produce on its screen every single color that exists in nature. Instead, computers use a combination of three primary colors. These primary colors are red, green and blue. Computers also use additive colors which are colors created by adding different levels of RGB.

RGB

RGB stands for red, green, blue --- the three primary colors. RGB follows the RGB color model. The color model uses numbers to represent how much of each primary color is displayed. This is how you format the RGB color model:

```
(R, G, B)
```

If you want the strongest red and no other color, you'd write the maximum amount of red and keep the other values zero. Like this:

```
(255, 0, 0)
```

Likewise, you can have either the strongest green:

```
(0, 255, 0)
```

Or the strongest blue:

```
(0, 0, 255)
```

But it doesn't mean you are limited to three colors only. You can use different values ranging from 0 to 255 to create many different colors. Here's an example:

```
(147, 112, 219)
```

The above RGB values will give you this color:

colormode()

If you use these RGB color values, you first need to change the color mode of the screen object using the **colormode()** function before you change the background color. The code will look like this:

```
turtle.Screen().colormode(255)
turtle.Screen().bgcolor(147, 112, 219)
```

And your turtle graphics window should look like this:

Isn't that cool? But why is 255 the limit? Well, the answer is in the extra learning right below!

EXTRA LEARNING: THE RGB LIMIT

The RGB limit is 255 because of the way computers store information. Computers use ones and zeros to process data. The smallest unit of data a computer can hold is a bit —- short for binary digit. A bit is either a one or zero. If you have eight bits you will get a byte. A byte is another unit of data that represents information such as letters or numbers. One byte is exactly equal to one RGB value. In 8-bit binary, the RGB value 0 is equal to 00000000 and the RGB value 255 is equal to 11111111. The amount of data stored in a byte translates to the RGB value. Since one RGB value is equal to a byte, this translates exactly to the value 255.

The Hexadecimal System

The **hexadecimal system** is another color system besides the RGB color model. You may have heard of it before. It is a number system that uses 16 characters to represent values.

These are 0,1,2,3,4,5,6,7,8,9,A,B,C,D,E, and F. In other words, the hexadecimal system is considered a base-16 number system. We humans use the base-10 system ---- the numbers zero to nine represent numbers. The hexadecimal system saves memory space while allowing the computer to store more information compared to the base-10 system.

This system creates a 6-digit hexadecimal color. See the difference, the three RGB values are for example:

> (147, 112, 219)

Hexadecimal translates that RGB into this 6-digit color code: #9370DB. Hexadecimal colors start with a hashtag # to tell the computer that it is a hexadecimal number.

Here is a chart that shows the contrast between the RGB and hexadecimal systems:

RGB base10	Hex base16	RGB base10	Hex base16
0	0	11	B
1	1	12	C
2	2	12	D
3	3	14	E
4	4	15	F
5	5	16	10
6	6	100	64
7	7	200	C8
8	8	250	FA
9	9	255	FF
10	A		

Little Cute Turtle in a Cool Jungle

Well, you sure had a ride in the world of computer color. It's time to head back to the cute little turtle. Now that you know how to use RGB colors, you can create a better blue background for your pet turtle.

First, you need to change the color mode of the *Screen()* object into RGB mode. To do this, use the *colormode()* function. Note that its parameter must be 255 for it to function properly. Write it this way:

```
turtle.Screen().colormode(255)
```

Alright, the screen is ready! Now when you want the computer to use RGB to create colors, use the *bgcolor()* function introduced earlier. But instead of 'light green' as the parameter, use RGB values.

The following values should create a shade of green:

```
(16, 69, 13)
```

Then you write the code like this:

```
turtle.Screen().bgcolor(16, 69, 13)
```

And press Enter. Now your turtle has a cool jungle background!

The complete code should look like this in IDLE Shell:

```
IDLE Shell 3.10.0
>>>
>>>
>>> import turtle
>>> turtle.shape('turtle')
>>> turtle.Screen().setup(300,300)
>>> turtle.Screen().colormode(255)
>>> turtle.Screen().bgcolor(16,69,13)
>>>
>>>
                                    Ln: 13  Col: 0
```

And your turtle graphics window should show a cool background color like this:

Unfortunately, the turtle is black and cannot be easily seen in the green jungle! Fortunately you can fix that by changing the turtle's color!

The Turtle Gets a New Color

Ok, think about the color you want your turtle to be. How about a red turtle! Awesome right? No? Well, at least give it a try anyway.

color()

The code for this is easy. Use the **color()** function that comes in the turtle module. This is what it looks like:

```
turtle.color(255, 0, 0)
```

Here's what that code does: it uses the *turtle* module, calls the module's *color()* function, then uses RGB values as parameters.

Actually, you don't need to follow the colors in this book, feel free to change it to your liking!

Your red turtle should look like this in the graphics window:

Wait! Red doesn't seem to blend well with blue. Try changing the turtle's color to white!

```
turtle.color(255, 255, 255)
```

pencolor()

Give your turtle an outline so you can see it even better. You can do this by using the **pencolor()** function!

```
turtle.pencolor(255, 0, 0)
```

Your turtle should look like this now:

Well, you can say that your turtle looks very cool. But the turtle looks quite small, so go ahead change its size!

The Giant Turtle

The turtle looks small for its jungle home and it is quite hard to see. You can change your turtle's size by using the **turtlesize()** function.

```
turtle.turtlesize(12, 12, 4)
```

turtlesize()

This function uses three parameters that determine the turtle's size. The first two values determine the stretch of the turtle (length and width). You can have a stretched turtle using these parameter values:

```
turtle.turtlesize(11, 18, 4)
```

Or have a fat turtle using these parameter values:

```
turtle.turtlesize(18, 11, 4)
```

The third parameter determines the size of the turtle's outline. You will learn more about the outline later.

resizemode()

If you want to reset the size of your turtle, because you somehow didn't like the way it looks, you can use the **resizemode()** function as shown below:

```
turtle.resizemode('auto')
```

The 'auto' parameter tells the function to resize the turtle back to its original size.

Right now, your turtle looks either a bit too big or too small. You can resize it to a reasonable size for its little habitat:

```
turtle.turtlesize(5, 5, 3)
```

Perfecto! Now it's a good time to talk about the outline of the turtle. Why? Because there is a good shortcut to adjusting the outline of the turtle. This is how you can do just that:

```
turtle.turtlesize(outline = 12)
```

This is the result:

Whoa, that outline is too thick! Use number 5 for the outline:

```
turtle.turtlesize(outline = 5)
```

Great! Your pet turtle now has a cool home, a unique color scheme, and of a reasonable size!

Slow and Steady Goes the Turtle

Your pet turtle is chilling in the jungle. It is time to make the turtle move around and explore its habitat.

forward() and back()

You can move the turtle by using the turtle module's **forward()** and **back()** functions! Both of these functions take an integer as parameter. For example, if you wrote:

```
turtle.forward(100)
```

The turtle will move 100 pixels forward across the screen.

Now, move him backwards by 295 pixels:

```
turtle.back(295)
```

Important note: If you don't like to see the trail line that the turtle draws when it moves, you can hide it by using turtle.penup() function before moving the turtle. You will learn more about how to use this function soon.

Cool! You can move it left or right! But what if you want to move it up or down? Well, you need to use two more functions for that.

left() and right()

Imagine that you are walking down a hallway. There is a door on your left and you want to enter the room behind the door. The only way you can do that is by turning your body towards the door and then walking to the door to enter. That's what you will do to move your turtle up or down!

You can rotate, or turn, the turtle by using the **left()** or **right()** functions. Now, make your turtle turn left facing the top of the window:

```
turtle.left()
```

But wait, that alone won't work because the function needs a parameter.

The *left()* function takes one parameter. This parameter is the number of degrees to turn or how far you want the turtle to turn. If you turned 360 degrees in real life, you would spin in a complete circle. If you turned 180 degrees, just half of 360, you would end up facing the opposite direction. Easy, right?

To make the turtle turn left, use 90 as parameter (a quarter of a circle).

```
turtle.left(90)
```

Yay! Now you can use the forward function to move the turtle "up".

```
turtle.forward(95)
```

Then make it turn right and move forward.

```
turtle.right(90)
turtle.forward(120)
```

Your little turtle is having a blast! Now, make him explore the bottom corner of the screen. Your next code must make the turtle turn right and move forward (meaning "down").

```
turtle.right(90)
turtle.forward(190)
```

Yay! Your pet turtle can now move around in its home. If you'd like to keep playing with these functions, go ahead! You will be using these functions soon with more advanced code.

Doodling on Graphics

Creating a Pen

To draw you need a pen. To create a pen you need to create an instance of the *turtle* object named *pen*. Remember that an instance is a copy, so your variable *pen* gets a copy of all the functions of the turtle object. The following line of code will create a pen:

```
pen = turtle.Turtle()
```

To draw a line simply use the *forward()* function. Any time you move the pen, it automatically draws a line. Give it a try:

```
pen.forward(100)
```

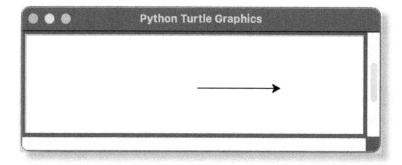

The line appears to be black, but you can fix that! You can change the pen color by using the *color()* function like the one you used earlier for your turtle.

```
pen.color('blue')
```

To see the color change, turn the pen and move it another 100 pixels:

```
pen.left(90)
pen.forward(100)
```

Here is the result:

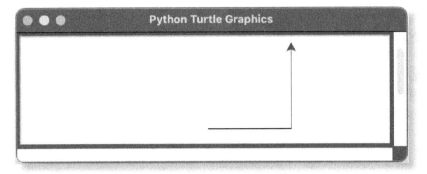

Yay! Now you are ready to create some shapes!

Creating a Shape

So it's time to create a shape! First, you will learn to draw a square. It is simple but you can show it off to your friends.

> *Note: It may be best to restart your IDLE Shell and redo the setup by first creating the pen instance. You may change the pen color at this point.*

Think of the color you might want for the square shape. This example use red to make a red square:

```
pen.color('red')
```

A square has four sides so you will need to create four lines. To begin, create a line of any length in pixel. The following examples use 100 pixels:

```
pen.forward(100)
```

This is the first side of the square. Guess what direction you need to go to create another side? Yup, a 90 degree turn. A square has 90 degree angles, or corners, that give it four equal sides.

To draw the second side of the square, rotate your pen then draw the second line with the same pixel length:

```
pen.left(90)
pen.forward(100)
```

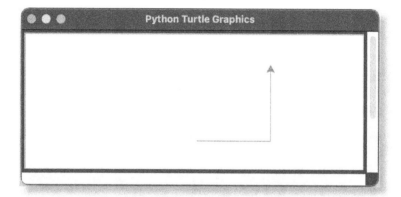

Congratulations! You finished drawing half of a square! Go ahead and draw the final two sides using the *left()* and *forward()* functions.

```
pen.left(90)
pen.forward(100)
pen.left(90)
pen.forward(100)
```

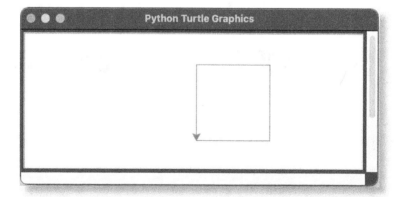

Did you get a square like the one shown above? Yes? Hooray! You made a red square!

hideturtle() or ht()

But wait, there is a leading arrow on the square! Well, that can be fixed by hiding the *pen* object. Using the special function *hideturtle()*, you can see the perfect square without the arrow. By the way, the function *hideturtle()* can be shortened to *ht()*.

```
pen.hideturtle()
```

Why is it called *hideturtle* you ask? Well, even though the object is called *pen*, it is an instance, or copy, of the turtle object. This means that all the names of the turtle functions remain the same.

Below is the perfect red square you created:

Here's what the complete code looks like in IDLE Shell:

```
>>>
>>> import turtle
>>> turtle.setup(250,250)
>>> pen = turtle.Turtle()
>>> pen.color('red')
>>> pen.forward(100)
>>> pen.left(90)
>>> pen.forward(100)
>>> pen.left(90)
>>> pen.forward(100)
>>> pen.left(90)
>>> pen.forward(100)
>>> pen.hideturtle()
>>>
```

Ln: 17 Col: 0

Did you notice something when you created the square? Exactly, you repeated two functions with the same parameters. Do you know what code can repeat those two functions in a loop? That's right, a *for loop*!

CHAPTER ACTIVITY: A Square Program

You can write a simple program that creates a square when you run it. Here's how you can do it:

First, make a new file. You can name the file anything, but for the following example name the file as *squareGraphics*. Next, import the turtle module and set up the pen. You can choose any color you prefer.

```
import turtle
pen = turtle.Turtle()
pen.color('red')
pen.ht()
```

ht is short for hideturtle

Create a for loop that will repeat four times:

```
for i in range(4):
    pen.forward(100)
    pen.left(90)
```

Altogether, your program should look like this:

```
import turtle
pen = turtle.Turtle()
pen.color('red')
pen.ht()
for i in range(4):
    pen.forward(100)
    pen.left(90)
```

Run the file and see the result!

Filling a Shape with Color

You have a cool program that draws a square but it only draws the sides. You can fill the empty space in the square with color using the *fillcolor()* function.

fillcolor()

This function will set the color that you want to fill the shape with. Its parameter is the color that you want.

```
pen.fillcolor('red')
```

begin_fill()

The next function to use is *begin_fill()*. It commands the computer to start filling the square with the selected color. This function is written before drawing the shape and doesn't require a parameter.

```
pen.begin_fill()
```

end_fill()

The final function to use is *end_fill()*. This function does not require a parameter. It signals that you are finished drawing and the computer will fill in the shape. Simple as that!

```
pen.end_fill()
```

You can play around with these functions in the square program that you wrote earlier. Here's what the code should look like if you wrote it correctly:

```python
import turtle
pen = turtle.Turtle()
pen.color('red')
pen.ht()
pen.fillcolor('red')

pen.begin_fill()
for i in range(4):
    pen.forward(100)
    pen.left(90)
pen.end_fill()
```

Run the above code and you will get this red square:

Turtle's Built-In Functions

The turtle has more functions! Learn and use them to write interesting programs. Before playing with the following functions, it may be best to reset your IDLE Shell (close the shell then restart Python). Then import turtle, create a pen, and hide the turtle.

```
import turtle
pen = turtle.Turtle()
pen.ht()
```

Now you're ready to learn and play with more turtle functions.

write()

The *write()* function works just like how it is named, it writes text! Similar to the *print()* function, it requires a string as a parameter. Use the *write()* function with any text you want to write!

```
pen.write("Hello World!")
```

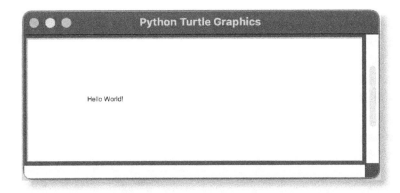

The words look tiny though. This is the default setting of the text. You can change the font by adding another parameter to the function. This parameter requires three values. First is for the text font, second is for the font size, and third is for the type. The type can be *normal*, *bold*, or *italicized*.

Try rewriting the line with these parameter values:

```
pen.write("Hello World!",font=('courier',40,'bold'))
```

clear()

The *clear()* function erases whatever is written or drawn on the screen. It requires no parameter.

```
pen.clear()
```

circle()

This cool function can draw circles! The *circle()* function can take up to three parameters: radius, extent, and steps. All of these parameters are integer data types.

```
pen.circle(radius, extent, steps)
```

The radius is half the diameter of the circle. You can try it now:

```
pen.circle(70)
```

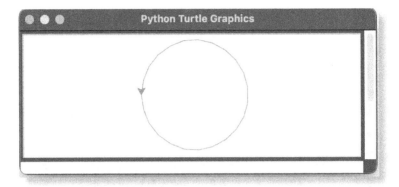

Cool! You got a circle with a radius of 70. If you add a second parameter, that parameter determines the extent the circle is drawn in degrees. Go ahead and create one half of a circle, or a semi-circle (one half of a circle has 180 degrees).

```
pen.clear()
pen.circle(70, 180)
```

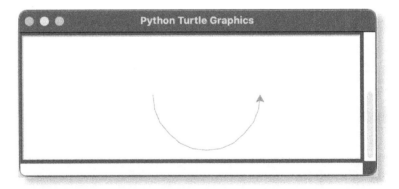

The third parameter is the steps, or the number of times the pen turns. You can change the number of steps the pen draws, so for example try drawing a complete circle (360 degrees) with just 3 steps:

```
pen.clear()
pen.circle(70, 360, 3)
```

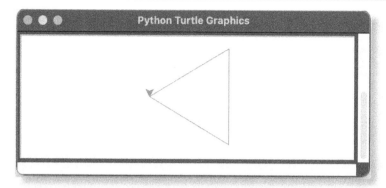

Whoops! It appears that you have created a triangle. But by increasing the value of the steps parameter you can create different results. It is time to experiment! This time try 10 steps:

```
pen.clear()
pen.circle(70, 360, 10)
```

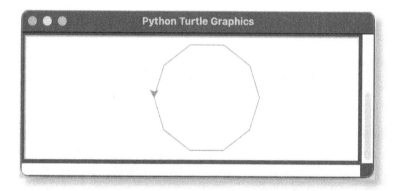

stamp() and penup()

Another fun function is the *stamp()*. It will stamp, or "imprint", the shape onto the screen. For example, first create a new copy of the turtle object and give it some basic settings. Then hide the line that the turtle draws when moving by using the *penup()* function.

```
newturtle = turtle.Turtle()
newturtle.shape('turtle')
newturtle.color('green')
newturtle.penup()
```

Now use the *stamp()* function then move it forward to reveal the copy!

```
newturtle.stamp()
newturtle.forward(100)
```

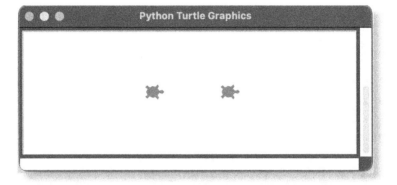

Wow! Got any ideas on how to use it? Make a loop of course!

MINI CHAPTER ACTIVITY: Turtle Stamps

Create a new file and name it anything you want. Start the code with the import of the turtle module and set it up however you want.

Here's an example setup:

```
import turtle
myturtle = turtle.Turtle()
myturtle.shape('turtle')
myturtle.color('blue')
myturtle.penup()
```

Use a *for loop* to repeat the following commands: turtle go forward, turtle stamp, turtle turn right. To make it interesting, experiment with different degree and loop values to create a circle of stamps.

Once you have completed and ran the code, you may see a shape like this:

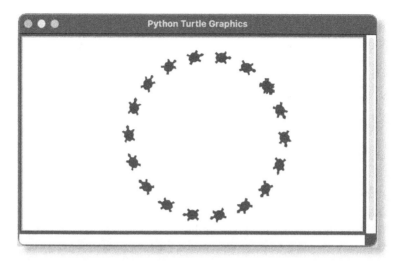

If you are stuck, you can go to the Chapter Solutions section at the end of the book for a sample solution code.

You have learned how to use the Turtle Module! You have created a turtle object, edited it, and made it move! You can draw shapes and use other built-in functions to create impressive patterns!

Chapter 6 Quick Review

Using Turtle

You learned:
- how to import the Turtle Module.
- how to use the Screen and Turtle Objects when you set up the module.
- how to interact with the Screen and Turtle Objects.
- how to turn the turtle object into a turtle shape.
- how to change the color of the screen and turtle objects.
- how to change the size of the turtle object.

RGB and Hexadecimal

You learned:
- that RGB is a color system using three values: Red, Green, and Blue.
- how to change the color system in RGB.
- how computers store information using bits and bytes.
- how to use RGB to change the color of the turtle object.
- the Hexadecimal color system which follows a base-16 system.

Moving the Turtle

You learned:
- how to use the *forward()*, *back()*, *left()*, and *right()* functions.
- how degrees affect the turn distance
- how to use pixels as a value to move the turtle object.

Creating Shapes

You learned:
- how to create an instance, or copy, of the turtle object.
- how to draw shapes
- how to use functions such as *ht()*, *penup()*, and *pendown()*
- how to create a program using a loop to draw a square.

Using In-Built Functions

You learned:
- how to use the *write()* function.
- how to use the *clear()* function.
- how to use the *circle()* function
- the circle's three parameters: radius, extent, and steps.
- how to use the *stamp()* function.
- how to create a circle of stamps.

Chapter 6 Activities

Activity #1: Colorful Turtles

Do you like spinning turtles? Do you also like turtles that change colors? Well, this activity is for you!

Write a program that will create a turtle-shaped object and change the color of the turtle after spinning 360 degrees. Use RGB values for the different colors!

Hint: Use a list to store the RGB values. This list will be the group of items used in a *'for loop'* to change to colors as well as rotating the turtle. Turn to page 111 as a reference for *'for loops'*.

Activity #2: Rainbow Spectrum

Yes! Rainbows! In this activity, you will write a program that draws a rainbow spectrum ---- a line of colors of the rainbow.

To draw this, make the pen size big, like very big. You can change the pen size using the *pensize()* function. For example:

```
pen.pensize(200)
```

Use a *for loop* that will move the pen some distance, change the color, draw the color, and repeat until all the colors have been drawn! Here's a sample list of colors:

```
rainbow_colors = ['red', 'yellow', ' green', 'blue', 'indigo', 'violet']
```

As an extra challenge, set the background screen to black to make the color spectrum stand out!

Activity #3: RGB Squares

This activity involves new functions and a lot of code to write. I am confident that you are up to the challenge, so go ahead!

In this activity, you will write a program that draws three squares with the colors: red, green, and blue! Sounds simple? Not so much. Additionally, you need to draw the squares separately.

To do this, you'll need to make three copies of the turtle object and set them up according to its color.

Here's a little help: To make it easier to position the squares on the window, you can choose to use the following functions:

.setposition() will set the position of the object using integers for its x and y coordinates. This takes two parameters, one for the *x coordinate* and one for the *y coordinate*, for example:

    square.setposition(300, 250)

If you want to know in which coordinates the current object is currently positioned, you can use the following functions: **xcor()** and **ycor()**.

.xcor() will return the object's *x coordinate*

For example:

    print(square.xcor())

.ycor() will return the object's *y coordinate*.

For example:

    print(square.ycor())

Stuck on any of the activities? Go to Chapter Solutions to see samples of code for each activity.

Chapter 7

Functions and Arguments

You will learn reusing code, functions, arguments, and return value

In this chapter, you will learn how to reuse code using functions, using arguments in functions, and returning values.

Concept of Reusability

At the core of code is the concept of reusability. The concept of reusability is the idea of using code over and over again. We write code that is complex and time consuming. Writing it over and over again is repetitive and isn't very useful. Functions allow you to overcome this. With functions, you are able to type code once and reuse it in a simpler and faster way.

Functions

As said earlier, functions are reusable blocks of code that can either do a specific task or return a value. You can write functions for code that you need to reuse.

To illustrate, say you wanted to greet someone. You can use the *print()* function to do this.

```
print("Hello, person!")
```

You can use the above code whenever you need to greet someone.

```
print("Hello, person!")
print("Hello, person!")
print("Hello, person!")
print("Hello, person!")
print("Hello, person!")
```

But as you see, writing the same line of code repeatedly is very time consuming and makes a messy code.

Instead, you can use a function to replace it.

```
def greet():
        print("Hello, person!")
```

Writing a Function

To write a function, you first need to use the keyword **def** ---- *def* is short for the word define. Use *def* to "define" a function, or in other words create a function and its purpose. This keyword is signalling to Python that the block of code is a function ---- similar to an *if statement* or *loop*.

```
def
```

Afterwards, you need to give it a name. In the earlier example, you used *greet*. It's good practice to use a name that matches the purpose of the function so that anyone who reads your code can understand the purpose of the function.

```
def greet
```

Once you have given the function a name, add parentheses.

```
def greet()
```

Parentheses after the function's name hold the parameters that will be used within the function. For this example, you don't need any parameters so leave it empty.

To complete the definition of the function, add a colon. This colon, like *loops* and *if statements*, will indent the block of code that is a part of the function.

```
def greet():
        print("Hello, person!")
```

Calling a Function

To use a function, you need to call it. Calling a function is writing the name of the function and any arguments you want to input into it. Since you've already created a *greet()* function, use it as an example.

To call a function, simply write the function's name and a set of parentheses.

```
greet()
```

The set of parentheses is where you would add the argument or arguments. But since this function doesn't need any, keep it blank (you will learn how to use arguments soon).

After writing *greet()* you've just signaled that you want to use that function. Python will then run the block of code within the function. If you run the file, the output should be:

```
Hello, person!
```

You can call the function anytime you want.

```
greet()
Hello, person!
greet()
Hello, person!
greet()
Hello, person!
```

Define Function First

Another thing to know about functions is that functions must be **defined first before they are called**. From the beginning of this book, you may remember the way the computer reads code; starting from the first line, reading from left to right, and going down to the next line of code.

For now, you can ditch the "left to right" idea and focus on the "top down" idea. Since a computer reads code from top down, it will get confused and throw an error at you if you were to call a function that it hasn't read yet.

To get a clearer idea, you can imagine that you were reading a book. The book then mentions a character that you haven't learned about yet. It'll confuse you since the book expects you to already know the character when you haven't even read that part yet. In short, you can't do the following code:

```
greet()          ◄─────────  can't call a function
def greet():                 that was not defined
    print("Hello, person!")
```

Instead, you **define the function first**:

```
def greet():
    print("Hello, person!")
greet()          ◄─────────  This works!
```

Arguments

Imagine a situation. In this situation, you have a list of names of your friends. You want to iterate through the list and print a greeting for each friend using its name. Afterwards, you also want to print the name of your best friend. How can you do that? Well, first create your list, for example:

```
my_friends = ['Edmond', 'Walter', 'Bernard', 'Napoleon']
```

Since you want to iterate through the list use a *for loop*, for example:

```
for friend in my_friends:
```

Here you have two choices, you can either use a simple *print()* and print out the names or make your own function. Let's make a quick contrast; if you use the *print()* function, you would just use an *f-string* and write:

```
print(f"Hello, {friend}!")
```

But it will be complicated to single out and print the name of your best friend that way. So instead, use a function. Define the function this way:

```
def greet():
        print("Hello, person!")
```

Here's a problem with that function though. When you call that function, it will only print out "Hello, person!" with no friend's name. You need to find a way to pass the information (the friend's name) into the function.

This is where arguments come into play.

Sample Arguments

You can pass information into a function through **arguments**, or **args** for short. Arguments are variables defined and used in a function. They are placed between the parentheses of a function. Here is a sample of a function with arguments:

```
def compare(value_1, value_2):
```

This sample function has two arguments. Functions can have multiple arguments separated by a comma.

The *compare()* function above can take in two values as it has two arguments.

When you call this function, it will have two values between the parentheses. But the arguments wouldn't be seen when the function is called. The values replace the arguments.

For example:

```python
def compare(value_1, value_2):
    # some functional code

my_guess = int(input("Guess a number: "))
robot_guess = 40
compare(my_guess, robot_guess)
```

Arguments are placeholders for values to be passed into the function. The arguments are then used within the function for whatever tasks. Here's an example of a functional task within the function:

```python
def compare(value_1, value_2):
    if value_1 > value_2:
        #additional code
```

Makes sense, right? Arguments are useful for when you need to pass information to the function.

Here is the complete code where the function prints out the result of your guess:

```python
def compare(value_1, value_2):
    if value_1 > value_2:
        print("You guessed higher!")

my_guess = int(input("Guess a number: "))
robot_guess = 40
compare(my_guess, robot_guess)
```

Now that you know the basics of arguments, you can solve the problem with the earlier *greet()* function.

Arguments can have any name, just like a variable. They don't need to be labeled *value_1* but can be *itemOne* or *unnecessarilyLongArgument*. They just need to match the value they are receiving.

For the *greet()* function, add an argument called 'name'

```
def greet(name):
    print("Hello, person!")
```

To make this function work, modify the *print()* line and add the argument 'name' into it:

```
def greet(name):
    print("Hello, " + name)
```

Now that you have the modified *the greet()* function, you can complete the rest of the code. The complete code should look like this:

```
my_friends = ['Edmond', 'Walter', 'Bernard', 'Napoleon']

def greet(name):
    print("Hello, " + name)

for friend in my_friends:
    greet(friend)

greet(my_friends[2])
```

this line solves the best friend problem

Run the code and you should see something like this:

```
Hello, Edmond
Hello, Walter
Hello, Bernard
Hello, Napoleon
Hello, Bernard
```

Bernard is the best friend

Parameters or Arguments

Parameters and arguments have the same purpose: passing information into a function.

```python
def greet(name): # "name" is an Argument
def greet(name): # "name" is also a Parameter
```

But they can be distinguished when defining a function. Below is the function's perspective:

Function's Perspective

• A parameter is the variable listed inside the parentheses of a function definition.
• An argument is the value that is passed into the function when called.

Returning Values

Functions are great but something important is still missing. Since functions are just reusable blocks of code you can do a lot with it besides printing out a string.

What if you want to call a function that adds two values? And instead of printing the value, you want to receive the final value back so you can use it within other parts of your code?

You want the function to return a value. This can be done easily with the return statement. Here's a sample code:

```python
def add(int_one, int_two):
    final_num = int_one + int_two
    return final_num
```

Here, you have a function called "add" with two parameters; *int_one* and *int_two*. Inside the function, the two values are added together. In the final line the *return* statement returns the final value of *final_num*.

CONGRATULATIONS!

Great! You learned functions!

Chapter 7 Quick Review

Functions

You learned:

- that functions are reusable blocks of code.
- that functions can either do a specific task or return a value or both.
- how to write a function using the keyword *def*.
- how to call a function using its name with a pair of parentheses.
- that functions need to be defined before it is called.

Arguments

You learned that:

- arguments, or *args*, is where data is be passed into a function.
- arguments are declared within the parentheses of a function.
- arguments are placeholders for values that are passed into the function so the function can use the values.
- parameters and arguments have the same purpose: passing data into a function.
- from a function's perspective, a parameter is the variable declared inside of the parentheses and an argument is the data passed into the function when it is called.

Chapter 7 Activities

Activity #1: Memory Greeting

In this exercise, the computer needs to greet two people. One person has never met the computer while the other has. Write a function that will take in two arguments, one is the name and other will be a boolean. Use two *if statements* to check if the person has met the computer or not. Print a different greeting for each *if statement*.

Here's a sample output:

```
Hello, John Doe, I am the computer!

Welcome back, Alfred!
```

Activity #2: Calculator

In this exercise, you will create a calculator! Each operation; addition, subtraction, etc, will be defined with functions. For division, check if the second value is not a zero, because you cannot divide by zero.

In every function, return the final value. Print out the values in *f-strings*.

Here's a sample code and output:

```
print(f"Addition: {add(5, 6)}")
print(f"Subtraction: {subtract(123, 54)}")
print(f"Multiplication: {multiply(4, 43)}")
print(f"Division: {divide(5, 0)}")
print(f"Division: {divide(20, 4)}")
Addition: 11
Subtraction: 84
Multiplication: 172
Division: Cannot Divide by 0
Division: 5.0
```

Chapter 8

Modules and Challenges

MODULES

Importing Python Modules

from import

This statement will import a specific attribute from a specific file. In other words, only one function/attribute is being imported, not the entire file.

Example:

```
from random import randint
```

import as

This statement will import a file but use it under a different name. This is useful for renaming long file names when they are imported.

Example:

```
import verylongfilenamefile as vlfn
```

The *from import* statement also works with *as*. Here's an example:

```
from time import sleep as wait
```

Random Module

The random module is used for generating random data. Two useful functions included in the random module are *randint()* and *choice()*.

randint()

It will generate a random value from a range of numbers. The range is defined by its two parameters.
For example:

```
import random

print(random.randint(1,20))
```

choice()

It will choose a random option. The options are passed to it as a parameter.
For example:

```
import random

print(random.choice(['Kingdom', 'Dynasty', 'Empire']))
```

Note that the options/parameter must be of the type list or it will not work.

Time Module

The time module contains useful functions related to time. A very common function is the *sleep()* function. This function will temporarily pause the code. The parameter it takes in is an integer or float, and this parameter is counted in seconds.

sleep()

For example:

```
import time
print("Welcome to the Game!")
time.sleep(1)   #Pauses code for 1 second
name = input("What is your name? "))
```

CHALLENGES

Challenge #1: **Random Lines**
(Difficulty: Medium)

Can you create a program using the Turtle Module that draws random lines in random directions?

Requirements:
• At least two lines with distinct colors.
• At least two lines that go in different directions.

Extra Challenge #1: Can you make your code more advanced by allowing the user to change the randomness of the lines?

Challenge #2: **Rock Paper Scissors**
(Difficulty: Medium to Advanced)

Can you create a Rock, Paper, Scissors game? The player will be playing the game against the computer program itself.

Requirements:
• Random Module is used for the computer.
• A function that compares the player's choice and computer's choice.
• Be able to play continuously.
• Prints out the winner of the game.

Extra Challenges:
- Player can can choose own name.
- Player can choose how many rounds to play.
- Program prints "3 2 1 Go!"
- Prints out the round number after every game played.
- Scoreboard
- Show final results after game has ended.
- Program can handle errors in input.

Helpful Tips:
- Use the time module for the pause effect.
- When using a *while loop*, use the keyword *break* to stop/escape the while loop.
- Make it so that the player has to type the number of the option instead of typing the full word.

Example:
Instead of "Rock, Paper, or Scissors?"
do "[1]Rock, [2]Paper, or [3]Scissors?"

Challenge #3: **Random Colorful Stars**
(Difficulty: Medium)

Can you create a program that draws randomly colorful stars using the Turtle Module?

Requirements:
- Random Module is used.
- A function that generates a random RGB color.
- At least two stars drawn.
- Stars must be colorful.

Extra Challenges:
- Star's pen size and length are random.
- The color of star rays is random.
- Stars are wobbling randomly.

Helpful Tips:
Use the functions *xcor()* and *ycor()* to help setting up positions.
Use a *while loop* to continuously draw stars.

For example:

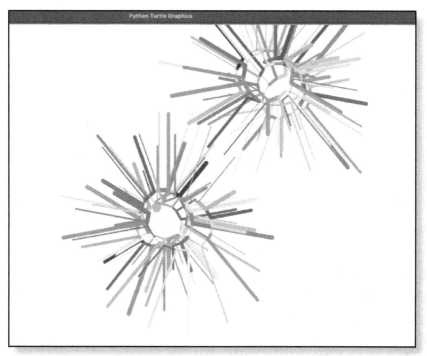

Challenge #4: RPG Program
(Difficulty: Medium to Advanced)

Can you create an RPG Simulation? An RPG is officially called a role playing game. Most common RPGs evolve around the system of killing monsters and earning rewards to upgrade. For this challenge, write a program in which the player types in commands that allows him to fight and see his stats.

Requirements:
• Commands that allow the player to: see his stats (money), fight monsters, and read instructions on how to play. Here are some commands that you can use:

    _help
    _fight
    _stats
    _commandlist

- Different monsters with different rewards that are randomly generated
- Money/Coin System

Helpful Tips:

- Keep notes of the values of each monster.
- Use separate functions for fighting, checking commands, and any other actions.
- Use a *while loop* to have a continuous input.
- Generate the random values of the monsters in the *while loop* to allow it to randomly generate after every action.
- Use a global statement for variables such as currency (A global statement allows a variable to be used inside and outside of a function. For Example: global coins)
- For commands, use *if statements* that check the command. If a command has two parts, use the *in operator* with a string condition.
- To help with variables and strings, use the *.format()* method. Write a pair of curly brackets that are empty in the code. *.format()* is written at the end of the string with the parameters of the variables.

Here is an example:

```python
print("You had slain a {} and got {} {}!".format(monster_slain, reward, monster_token))
```

Every pair of curly brackets is a parameter for the method.
Use a list to check for the monster that is randomly generated.

Extra Challenges:

Create a command that allows the player to 'visit' a shop and buy equipment such as weapons or armor.

Although difficult, it is possible to add a leveling system using *if statements* to check for XP after every fight.

Challenge #5: Colorful Bouncing Ball
(Difficulty: Hard to Advanced)

Can you create a ball bouncing off the inner walls of a square?

Requirements:
• A square at least 500 pixels large.
• Large enough for the ball to bounce around inside.
• The ball should change its color after every bounce.
• The ball must not go outside the square.

Helpful Tips:
• Use the turtle and random modules.
• Create two instances of the turtle object, one for the square and the other for the ball.
• Use the *xcor()* and *ycor()* methods.
• You can reuse the *create_color()* function from the challenge #3 sample solution.
• The Python default size of the ball object is 20 pixels.

For example:

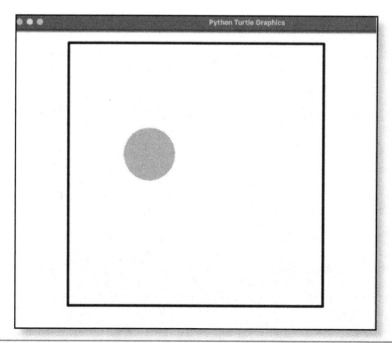

Challenge #6: Six Turtles Crossing a Highway
(Difficulty: Hard to Advanced)

Can you make six turtles that are crossing a highway?

Requirements:
- A highway must be drawn.
- The turtles must cross from one side of the highway to the other.
- Once a turtle reaches the other side, it will disappear and a new one will appear on the starting side.
- Turtles must vary randomly in sizes and colors.
- Outline colors must vary randomly.
- The speeds must vary randomly.

Hints:
- Use turtle and random modules.
- Use *setposition()*, *penup()*, and *pendown()* methods.
- Use *hideturtle()* or *ht()* or *showturtle()* or *st()* methods.
- Create 6 turtle objects.
- Create a pen to draw the highway.
- You can reuse the *create_color()* function from challenge #3 sample solution to generate random RGB values.

For example:

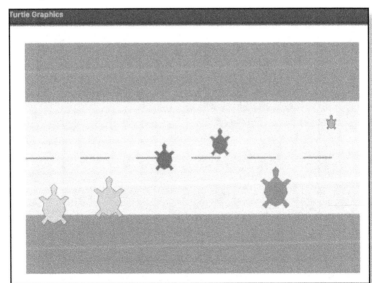

Challenge #7: Stopwatch
(Difficulty: Medium to Hard)

Can you create a stopwatch using the Turtle and Time modules?

Requirements:
• A stopwatch clock in text is shown on the Python Turtle Graphics window.
• The stopwatch must count by seconds, showing both minutes and seconds.
• Stopwatch must reset after time is up and start again.
• Stopwatch must be in a 12 Hour clock format. Example: 2:39

Helpful Tips:
• Use the turtle object function *clear()* to clear text.
• Write a variable for each digit instead of one variable being incremented. One variable for the single-digit seconds, another variable for the two-digit seconds, and one final one for the minutes.
• Use *if statements* to check each digits current integer and increment based on it.
• Use a *for loop* inside a *while loop*. A *for loop* for the stopwatch and the *while loop* for the time lapse.
• Allow the user to change the length of time lapse. Input for minutes and input for seconds, then convert into one final time length.

For example:

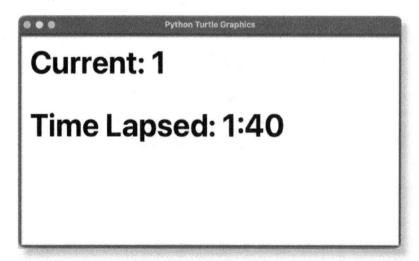

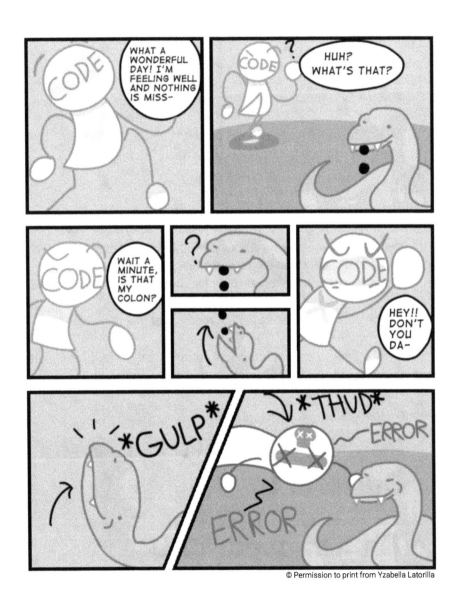

© Permission to print from Yzabella Latorilla

Chapter Solutions

Chapter 1

Chaper 1 - Exercise #1: Sample solution code

```python
print("Hello, how is your day going?")
```

Chaper 1 - Exercise #2: Sample solution code

```python
name = 'Roger'
country = 'Canada'
favorite_food = 'Pancakes'
print(f"Hi, my name is {name}, I am from {country} and my favorite food is {favorite_food}!")
```

Chaper 1 - Exercise #3: Sample solution code

```python
# a = "Person"
# print("a")

a = "Person"
print(a)
```

Chaper 1 - Exercise #4: Sample solution code

```python
print("""I don't know how to
Make a haiku okay? See,
I am bad at this
""")
```

Chaper 1 - Exercise #5: **Sample solution code**

```python
first_name = 'Jason'
last_name = 'L'
full_name = first_name + " " + last_name
print(full_name)
```

Chapter 2

Chaper 2 - Exercise #1: **Sample solution code**

```python
name = "Harry Potluck"
age = 10 + 4
print(f"Hi, my name is {name}!")
print("I am " + age + " years old.")
```

Chaper 2 - Exercise #2: **Sample solution code**

```python
my_float = 0
my_float += 192.165
my_float += 6.33
my_float += 12.005
my_float += 3.14159265358979323846264
print(my_float)
```

Chaper 2 - Exercise #3: **Sample solution code**

```python
my_number = 338
mysterious_number = 2021

print(f"Your number is greater than the mysterious number?
{my_number > mysterious_number}")
```

Chapter 3

Chaper 3 - Exercise #1: Sample solution code

```
animal = input("Name an animal: ")
name = input("Give a name: ")
adjective = input("Name an adjective: ")
food = input("Name a food: ")

print(f"""Once lived a {animal} called {name}. {name}
is {adjective} because he likes to eat {food}""")
```

Chaper 3 - Exercise #2: Sample solution code

```
secret_message = input("Your message: ")
message_length = len(secret_message)
print(f"The length of your secret message is: {message_length}")
```

Chaper 3 - Exercise #3: Sample solution code

```
test_answers = [False, True, True]

question_one = input("True or False: An apple is an orange? ")
question_two = input("True or False: Do you like cake? ")
question_three = input("True or False: The author is cool? ")

print(f"""
Your results:
Question One | Your Answer: {question_one} - Correct Answer:
{test_answers[0]}
Question Two | Your Answer: {question_two} - Correct Answer:
{test_answers[1]}
Question Three | Your Answer: {question_three} - Correct Answer:
{test_answers[2]}
""")
```

Chaper 3 - Exercise #4: Sample solution code

```python
test_answers = [False, True, True]
user_answers = []

question_one = input("True or False: An apple is an orange? ")
user_answers.append(question_one)
question_two = input("True or False: Do you like cake? ")
user_answers.append(question_two)
question_three = input("True or False: The author is cool? ")
user_answers.append(question_three)

print(f"Is the entire test correct? {test_answers == user_answers}")
```

Chaper 3 - Exercise #5: Sample solution code

```python
fruits = ('apple', 'banana', 'pear', 'grapes', 'peach')

guess = input("Name a fruit: ")
print(f"Is it a real fruit? {guess in fruits}")
```

Chapter 4

Chaper 4 - Exercise #1: Sample solution code

```python
password = 'cookies'

response = input("What is the password? ")
if response == password:
    print("Correct! You get free cookies!")
else:
    print("Sorry, that is not the correct password")
```

Chaper 4 - Exercise #2: Sample solution code

```
game_name = 'Story Game'
username = input("What is your name?  ")
print(f"Welcome, {username}, to {game_name}!")
user_choice = input("A man in a dark cloak approaches you and
asks you to follow him. \nWill you: [1]Follow or [2]Ignore  ")
if user_choice == '1':
    print("\n___YOU FOLLOW THE MAN___")
    user_choice = input("The man offers you a shiny gold key. \nWill
you [1]Take it or [2]Decline his offer  ")
    if user_choice == '1':
        print("\n___YOU ACCEPT THE OFFER___")
        print("The golden key suddenly teleports you into empty space.
You'll probably die out there.")
        print("THE END: You died!")
    else:
        print("\n___YOU DECLINE THE OFFER___")
        print("The man walks away.")
        print("THE END: You survived!")
else:
    print("\nWell the story ends here.")
```

Chaper 4 - Exercise #3: Sample solution code

```
correct_answers = ['europe', 'antarctica', 'asia']
answer_index = 0
score = 0

print("====WELCOME TO GEOGUESSR====")

#EUROPE - INDEX 0
```

Continued on next page...

Continuation of code

```python
print("""
You are in a city. A tall tower can be seen in the distance.
Some buildings have flags with red white and blue.
What continent are you on?""")
guess = input("YOUR GUESS: ")
if guess == correct_answers[answer_index]:
    score += 1
answer_index += 1


#ANTARCTICA - INDEX  1
print("""
You are in the middle of nowhere.
It's freezing and the environment you are in is full of snow and
glaciers.
There are penguins walking nearby.
What continent are you on?""")
guess = input("YOUR GUESS: ")
if guess == correct_answers[answer_index]:
    score += 1
answer_index += 1


#ASIA - INDEX 2
print("""
You are in a city with tall skyrises. People flood the streets.
There are many architectural feats nearby.
The signs are covered in language that uses symbols.
What continent are you on?""")
guess = input("YOUR GUESS: ")

if guess == correct_answers[answer_index]:
    score += 1
answer_index += 1

print(f"Your total score: {score} out of 3")

#end of code
```

Chapter 5

Chaper 5 - Exercise #1: Sample solution code

```python
score = 564
random_number = '564'
favorite_number = '28'

if str(score) == random_number:
    print("Yay!")

if int(favorite_number) == 28:
    print("Cool number!")
```

Chaper 5 - Exercise #2: Sample solution code

```python
person_traits = ['john doe', 'tall', 'science']
current_trait_num = 0

for trait in person_traits:
    if current_trait_num == 0:
        print(f"My name is {trait}")
    elif current_trait_num == 1:
        print(f"I am {trait}")
    else:
        print(f"My major is {trait}")
    current_trait_num += 1
```

Chaper 5 - Exercise #3: **Sample solution code**

```
#FOR LOOP VERSION
number = 9999999
for i in range(number):
    for x in range(number):
        print(x)
        number += 9999999


#WHILE LOOP VERSION
y = 0
while True:
    print(y)
    y += 1
```

Chaper 5 - Exercise #4: **Sample solution code**

```
number = 13
guess = 0

while guess != number:
    guess = int(input("\nPick a number between 0
and 20:  "))
  if guess == number:
    print("Correct!")
  elif guess < 1 or guess > 20:
    print("That is not a valid number. Try again.")
  elif guess > number:
    print("That number is too high. Try again.")
  elif guess < number:
    print("That number is too low. Try again.")
  else:
    print("That is not a valid answer. Try again.")
```

Chapter 6

Mini Chapter Activity: Turtle Stamps sample solution code

```python
import turtle

#setup
copy = turtle.Turtle()
copy.shape('turtle')
copy.color('blue')
copy.ht()
copy.penup()

#loop
for i in range(20):
    copy.forward(40)
    copy.stamp()
    copy.right(20)
```

Chaper 6 - Exercise #1: Sample solution code

```python
import turtle

#setup
turtle.setup(600, 600)
turtle.shape('turtle')
turtle.colormode(255)

RGB_List = [(255, 215, 0), (0, 191, 255), (240, 128, 128)]

for rgb in RGB_List:
    turtle.color(rgb)
    for i in range(4):
        turtle.left(90)
```

Chaper 6 - Exercise #2: Sample solution code

```python
import turtle
turtle.setup(800, 700)
turtle.Screen().bgcolor('black')

rainbow_colors = ['red', 'yellow', 'green', 'blue', 'indigo', 'violet']

pen = turtle.Turtle()
pen.ht()
pen.pensize(200)
pen.penup()
pen.back(300)

pen.pendown()
for color in rainbow_colors:
    pen.color(color)
    pen.forward(100)
```

Chaper 6 - Exercise #3: Sample solution code

```python
import turtle
turtle.setup(700, 400)

#second square aka middle
secondSquare = turtle.Turtle()
secondSquare.penup()
secondSquare.ht()
y = secondSquare.ycor()
x = secondSquare.xcor()
secondSquare.color('green')
secondSquare.fillcolor('green')
#first square aka left
firstSquare = turtle.Turtle()
firstSquare.penup()
```

Continued on the next page...

Continuation of code

```
firstSquare.ht()
firstSquare.setposition((x-200), y)
firstSquare.color('red')
firstSquare.fillcolor('red')

#third square aka right
thirdSquare = turtle.Turtle()
thirdSquare.penup()
thirdSquare.ht()
thirdSquare.setposition((x+200), y)
thirdSquare.color('blue')
thirdSquare.fillcolor('blue')

firstSquare.pendown()
secondSquare.pendown()
thirdSquare.pendown()

#create triple squares
firstSquare.begin_fill()
secondSquare.begin_fill()
thirdSquare.begin_fill()

for i in range(4):

    firstSquare.forward(100)
    secondSquare.forward(100)
    thirdSquare.forward(100)

    firstSquare.left(90)
    secondSquare.left(90)
    thirdSquare.left(90)

firstSquare.end_fill()
secondSquare.end_fill()
thirdSquare.end_fill()

#end of code
```

Chapter 7

Exercise #1: **Sample solution code**

```python
def greet(name, was_here):
    if not was_here:
        print(f"Hello, {name}, I am the computer!")
    else:
        print(f"Welcome back, {name}!")

#FUNC IF COMPUTER DOES NOT KNOW THE PERSON
greet("John Doe", False)

#FUNC IF COMPUTER KNOWS THE PERSON
greet("Alfred", True)
```

Chapter 7 - Exercise #2: **Sample solution code**

```python
def add(value1, value2):
    final_value = value1 + value2
    return final_value

def subtract(value1, value2):
    final_value = value1 - value2
    return final_value

def multiply(value1, value2):
    final_value = value1 * value2
    return final_value
```

Continued on the next page...

Continuation of code

```python
def divide(value1, value2):
    if value2 == 0:
        return "Cannot Divide by 0"
    else:
        final_value = value1 / value2
        return final_value
print(f"Addition: {add(5, 6)}")
print(f"Subtraction: {subtract(138, 54)}")
print(f"Multiplication: {multiply(4, 43)}")
print(f"Division: {divide(5, 0)}")
print(f"Division: {divide(20, 4)}")
#end of code
```

Chapter 8

Challenge #1: Random Lines
(Note: no sample solution to extra chalenge)

```python
import turtle
from random import randint, choice

#first instance
rd = turtle.Turtle()
rd.color('grey')
rd.ht()
rd.pensize(4)

#second instance
st = turtle.Turtle()
st.ht()
st.pensize(randint(1,5))
```

Continued on the next page...

Continuation of code

```python
#Minimum range value
MINVAL = 20

#Maximum range value
MAXVAL = 100

#Random Loop Value
RLV = randint(MINVAL, MAXVAL)


for i in range(RLV):
    rd.forward(randint(MINVAL, MAXVAL))
    st.forward(randint(MINVAL, MAXVAL))
    direction = choice([1, 2])
    if direction == 1:
        rd.left(randint(MINVAL, MAXVAL))
        st.left(randint(MINVAL, MAXVAL))
    elif direction == 2:
        rd.right(randint(MINVAL, MAXVAL))
        st.right(randint(MINVAL, MAXVAL))
    else:
        print("something went wrong")
#output when done
print('finished')


#end of code
```

Chapter 8 - Challenge #2: Rock Paper Scissors

NOTE: Not all of the code written here is necessary to playing the game. The code is long because it has multiple features added to the game.

```python
import random
import time

"""
___NOTES___
item1 = user
item2 = computer
1 = Rock
2 = Paper
3 = Scissors
"""

countdown = [3, 2, 1]
game = True
computerScore = 0
playerScore = 0

def score(player, computer):
    print(f"""
_____SCORE_____
  {playerName}: {player}
  Computer: {computer}
""")

def computer_move():
    c = random.choice([1, 2, 3])
    time.sleep(2)
    if c == 1:
        display = 'Rock'
    elif c == 2:
        display = 'Paper'
```

Continued on the next page...

Continuation of code

```python
    else:
        display = 'Scissors'
    print(f"\nComputer Chose \"{display}\"")
    return c

def compare(item1, item2):
    if item1 == item2:
        return 'tie'
    #ROCK
    elif item1 == 1:
        if item2 == 2:
            return 'computer'
        else:
            return 'player'
    #PAPER
    elif item1 == 2:
        if item2 == 1:
            return 'player'
        else:
            return 'computer'
    #SCISSORS
    elif item1 == 3:
        if item2 == 1:
            return 'computer'
        else:
            return 'player'
    else:
        return 'invalid'

print("Welcome to Rock, Paper, Scissors!")
time.sleep(.9)
playerName = input("What is your name? \nINPUT: ")

time.sleep(.9)
```

Continued on the next page...

Continuation of code

```python
rounds = int(input("How many rounds do you want to
play? \nINPUT: "))
print("Get ready to play in...", end=' ')
for i in countdown:
    time.sleep(1)
    print(str(i), end=' ')
time.sleep(1)
print("Go!")
time.sleep(1)

num_round = 1
valid_round = True
while True:
    if valid_round:
        print(f"\n_____ROUND {num_round}
_____")
        valid_round = False
    time.sleep(1)
    score(playerScore, computerScore)
    computerMoveClear = True
    move = int(input(f"{playerName}, [1]Rock,
[2]Paper, or [3]Scissors?\nINPUT:  "))
    if move > 3 or move < 1:
        print("\n____INVALID OPTION____")
        computerMoveClear = False
        time.sleep(2)
    if computerMoveClear:
        result = compare(move, computer_move())
        time.sleep(2)
        if result == 'player':
            print("Player Wins This Round!")
            num_round += 1
            playerScore += 1
            valid_round = True
            if num_round > rounds:
                break
```

Continued on the next page...

Continuation of code

```python
        elif result == 'tie':
            print("It's a tie! No one wins this
round.")
            num_round += 1
            rounds += 1
            valid_round = True
        elif result == 'computer':
            print("The Computer Wins This Round!")
            num_round += 1
            computerScore += 1
            valid_round = True
            if num_round > rounds:
                break
        else:
            print("Something went wrong...")

winner = 'No one won!'

if playerScore > computerScore:
    winner = f'{playerName} won the game!'
elif playerScore < computerScore:
    winner = 'The Computer won the game!'

print(f"""
_____FINAL RESULTS_____
    {playerName}: {playerScore}
    Computer: {computerScore}

{winner}
""")


#end of code
```

Chapter 8 - Challenge #3: Random Colorful Stars

```python
import turtle
import random

#create two pens
pen = turtle.Turtle()
pen2 = turtle.Turtle()

#move the second pen to upper right corner
pen2.penup()
pen2.setposition(pen.xcor()+300, pen.ycor()+300)
pen2.pendown()

#set the pen speed
pen.speed('fastest')
pen2.speed('fastest')

#some general settings
turtle.setup(1000,1000)
turtle.colormode(255)

#set the shape of the first pen
pen.shape('circle')

#define function to create random RGB values
def create_color():
    color_R = random.randint(0, 255)
    color_G = random.randint(0, 255)
    color_B = random.randint(0, 255)
    ret_RGB = (color_R, color_G, color_B)
    return ret_RGB
```

Continued on the next page...

Continuation of code

```python
#start the loop to draw
while True:
    #pen
    pen_size = random.randint(1, 10)
    ray_length = random.randint(50, 200)
    pen.color(create_color())
    pen.pensize(pen_size)

    pen.right(90)
    pen.forward(ray_length)
    pen.back(ray_length)
    pen.left(90)
    pen.left(20)
    pen.forward(random.randint(10, 30))

    #pen2
    pen_size2 = random.randint(1, 10)
    ray_length2 = random.randint(50, 200)
    pen2.color(create_color())
    pen2.pensize(pen_size2)

    pen2.right(90)
    pen2.forward(ray_length2)
    pen2.back(ray_length2)
    pen2.left(90)
    pen2.left(20)
    pen2.forward(random.randint(10, 30)))

#This sample code cannot stop by itself.
#To stop the program, you have to close
#the Python Turtle Graphics window.


#end of code
```

Chapter 8 - Challenge #4: RPG Game

```python
import random

#List of commands and their descriptions
cmds_list = {
    '_help': 'Explains how to play the simulation
and use commands',
    '_commandlist': 'Prints out the list of
Commands',
    '_help-cmd': 'Prints out the description of the
command',
    '_end': 'Stops the Simulation',
    '_fight': 'Command to Fight a monster',
    '_stats': 'Shows your stats',
    '_value': 'Shows your Character value'
    }

#default stats
copper_coins = 0
silver_coins = 0
gold_coins = 0

#Default Coins - Declare so it can be used
copper_value_monster = 10
silver_value_monster = 5
gold_value_monster = 3

#Dictionary of monster values. Mostly used as
#reference to show value of rewards
monster_values = {
    'Slime': copper_value_monster,
    'Spider': copper_value_monster,
    'Bat': copper_value_monster,
    'Wolf': silver_value_monster,
    'Giant Boar': silver_value_monster,
    'Giant Cobra': gold_value_monster
    }
```

Continued on the next page...

Continuation of code

```python
#List of monsters used in fight()
#for random choice

monster_list = ['Slime', 'Spider', 'Bat', 'Wolf',
'Giant Boar', 'Giant Cobra']

#Function to fight mobs a reward player

def fight():
    global copper_coins, silver_coins, gold_coins
    reward = 0
    monster_token = 'copper coins'
    monster_slain = random.choice(monster_list)

    #if a copper value monster is slain
    if monster_slain in ['Slime', 'Spider',
'Bat']:
        monster_token = 'copper coins'
        reward = copper_value_monster
        copper_coins += reward

    #if a silver value monster is slain
    elif monster_slain in ['Wolf', 'Giant Boar']:
        monster_token = 'silver coins'
        reward = silver_value_monster
        silver_coins += reward

    #if a gold value monster is slain
    elif monster_slain == 'Giant Cobra':
        monster_token = 'gold coins'
        reward = gold_value_monster
        gold_coins += reward
    print("You had slain a {} and got {}
{}!".format(monster_slain, reward,
monster_token))
```

Continued on the next page...

Continuation of code

```
#Function that checks for _help-cmd command and
#access command dictionary
def help_cmd(desc):
    if 'commandlist' in desc:
        print('_commandlist Command: ' +
cmds_list['_commandlist'])
    elif 'end' in desc:
        print('_end Command: ' + cmds_list['_end'])
    elif 'fight' in desc:
        print('_fight Command: ' +
cmds_list['_fight'])
    elif 'stats' in desc:
        print('_stats Command: ' +
cmds_list['_stats'])
    elif 'value' in desc:
        print('_value Command: ' +
cmds_list['_value'])
    else:
        print("Command does not exist.")


#checks player input for commands
def check(cmd):
    #checks for _ which is used in all commands
    if '_' in cmd:
        if cmd == '_help':
            print("____HOW TO PLAY____")
            print("""
    This is a Basic RPG Game.
    Use commands to do actions.
    Each command has '_' before the word. This indicates that it is
a command.
    Type '_commandlist' for a list of commands.
    Type '_help-cmd' to learn what a command does. Example:
'_help-cmd stats'
    Type '_fight' to begin fighting monsters.
    """)
```

Continued on the next page...

Continuation of code

```python
    elif cmd == '_commandlist':
        print("____AVAILABLE COMMANDS____")
        for command in cmds_list:
            print(f"{command}    ")
    elif '_help-cmd' in cmd:
        return 'hct'
    elif cmd == '_end':
        print("Simulation Ended")
        exit()
    elif cmd == '_stats':
        print(f"""
Copper Coins: {copper_coins}
Silver Coins: {silver_coins}
Gold Coins: {gold_coins}""")
    elif cmd == '_value':
        print(f"""
Total Amount of Coins:
{copper_coins+silver_coins+gold_coins}
   Copper: {copper_coins} | 1 Copper Coin = 1
Standard Value
   Silver: {silver_coins} | 1 Silver Coin = 5
Copper Coins or 5 Standard Values
   Gold: {gold_coins} | 1 Gold Coin = 10 Silver
Coins or 50 Standard Values
   Character Value: {copper_coins+
(silver_coins*5)+(gold_coins*50)}
   Your Character Value is measured in Standard
Values.
   """)
        elif cmd == '_fight':
            return 'f'
        else:
            print("Invalid Command!")
    else:
        print("Invalid Input. Perhaps you forgot _ ?")
```

Continued on the next page...

Continuation of code

```
#Greeting at start of game

print("Welcome to the Basic RPG Game!\nType
\'_help\' for instructions on how to play.")

#While Loop to keep regenerating monster's
#rewards and allow for
#input after every command

while True:

    #generate random value for each monster reward

    copper_value_monster = random.randint(5, 30)
    silver_value_monster = random.randint(4, 10)
    gold_value_monster = random.randint(2, 5)

    #Input for command. If check() function
    #returns data,
    #other functions are used

    user_cmd = input("COMMAND:  ")
    hc = check(user_cmd)
    if hc == 'hct':
        help_cmd(user_cmd)
    elif hc == 'f':
        fight()

    #Separation string to make output clean

    print("==================")


#end of code
```

Chapter 8 - Challenge #5: Colorful Bouncing Ball

```python
#bouncing ball challenge

import turtle
import random

#set color mode to RGB
turtle.colormode(255)

ballsize = 5
#set the offset nr for ball size
#the default size of object is 20 pixels
#the default radius is 10 pixels
#add 6 to the radius for safe offset
balloffset = (ballsize * 10) + 4

#make pen and ball
pen = turtle.Turtle()
pen.speed('fastest')
pen.ht()

ball = turtle.Turtle()
ball.shape('circle')
ball.turtlesize(ballsize)
ball.penup()
ball.speed('fastest')

#set square size
squaresize = 500
```

Continued on the next page...

Continuation of code

```python
#move the pen to left bottom corner
pen.penup()
pen.right(225)
pen.forward(squaresize)
pen.left(135)
pen.pendown()

#store the xy bounds
xleft = int(pen.xcor())
xright = int(xleft + squaresize)
ybottom = int(pen.ycor())
ytop = int(ybottom - squaresize)


#define function to check if ball is
#outside square
def outsidesquare(x, y, offset):
    xl =  x - offset
    x +=  offset
    yt =  y + offset
    y -=  offset

    if x >= xright or y <= ytop or xl <= xleft
or yt >= ybottom:
        #if outside pull back a bit
        ball.back(3)
        return True
    else:
        return False
```

Continued on the next page...

Continuation of code

```python
#define function to create random RGB values
def create_color():
    color_R = random.randint(0, 255)
    color_G = random.randint(0, 255)
    color_B = random.randint(0, 255)
    ret_RGB = (color_R, color_G, color_B)
    return ret_RGB

#create the square
pen.pensize(5)
for i in range(4):
    pen.forward(squaresize)
    pen.left(90)

#bounce the ball around inside square

while True:
    #get current position
    x = ball.xcor()
    y = ball.ycor()

    if outsidesquare(x,y, balloffset):
        newdirection = random.randint(45,90)
        ball.right(newdirection)
        #change the ball color after every bounce
        ball.color(create_color())

    ball.forward(4)

#This sample code cannot stop by itself.
#To stop the program, you have to close
#the Python Turtle Graphics window.

#end of code
```

Chapter 8 - Challenge #6: Turtles Crossing a Highway

```
#6 turtles crossing a highway

import turtle
import random

turtle.ht()
turtle.shape('turtle')

#length of highway in pixels
hwysize = 600
#y coord of starting position
y_upstart = 50
#y coord of end position
y_upend = 350
#x coords of x positions
x_starts = (50, 150, 250, 350, 450, 550)

#create the pen for highway
pen = turtle.Turtle()
pen.pensize(3)
pen.ht()
pen.speed(0)

#create an empty list for storing turtles
t = []

#function to draw highway rectangles
def drawrect(x,y,c):
    pen.color(c)
    pen.pendown()
    for i in range(2):
        pen.forward(x)
        pen.left(90)
        pen.forward(y)
        pen.left(90)
    pen.penup()
```

Continued on the next page...

Continuation of code

```python
#function to create random RGB values
def create_color():
    color_R = random.randint(0, 255)
    color_G = random.randint(0, 255)
    color_B = random.randint(0, 255)
    ret_RGB = (color_R, color_G, color_B)
    return ret_RGB

#function to draw the highway
def drawhighway():
    #draw the main lanes
    pen.fillcolor('yellow')
    pen.penup()
    pen.setposition(0,100)
    pen.begin_fill()
    drawrect(hwysize,200,('yellow'))
    pen.end_fill()

    #draw side walks
    pen.fillcolor('gray')
    pen.setposition(0,0)
    pen.begin_fill()
    drawrect(hwysize,100,('gray'))
    pen.setposition(0,300)
    drawrect(hwysize,100,('gray'))
    pen.end_fill()

    #draw the center line
    pen.setposition(0,200)
    pen.color('red')
    pen.pensize(3)
    for i in range(6):
        pen.pendown()
        pen.forward(50)
        pen.penup()
        pen.forward(50)
```

Continued on the next page...

Continuation of code

```python
#function to init turtle position
def start_turtle(tx,xpos):
    t[tx].ht()
    t[tx].penup()
    t[tx].setposition(xpos,y_upstart)
    t[tx].speed(random.randint(0,10))
    t[tx].turtlesize(random.randint(1,3))
    t[tx].color(create_color())
    t[tx].pencolor(create_color())

#function to move turtle
def moveturtle(tx):
    t[tx].st()
    if t[tx].ycor() >= y_upend:
        t[tx].ht()
        start_turtle(tx,x_starts[tx])
        t[tx].st()
    else:
        t[tx].forward(random.randint(3,7))

#switch the colormode
turtle.colormode(255)

#create highway
drawhighway()

#create six turtles
for i in range(6):
    t.append(turtle.Turtle())
    t[i].ht()
    t[i].penup()
    t[i].shape('turtle')
    t[i].left(90)
```

Continued on the next page...

Continuation of code

```python
#initialize all turtles
for i in range(len(t)):
    start_turtle(i,x_starts[i])

#draw the turtles crossing

while True:
    i = random.randint(0,len(t)-1)
    moveturtle(i))

#This sample code cannot stop by itself.
#To stop the program, you have to close
#the Python Turtle Graphics window.

#end of code
```

Chapter 8 - Challenge #7: Stopwatch

```python
from time import sleep as wait
import turtle

#video length variable inputs
minutes = int(input("Minutes:  "))
seconds = int(input("Seconds:  "))
start = input("Type 1 to begin:  ")

#Clock Counter Text
turtle.setup(700, 700)
clock_counter = turtle.Turtle()
clock_counter.ht()
clock_counter.penup()
clock_counter.setposition(-300, 0)

#Current Time Lap Text
current_loop = turtle.Turtle()
current_loop.ht()
current_loop.penup()
current_loop.setposition(-300, 100)

#variables that will be incremented
current = 1
lapsed_seconds = 0
lapsed_tensSeconds = 0
lapsed_minutes = 0
stat = False

#convert minutes to seconds and add seconds for
#total time
vid_length = seconds + (minutes * 60)

#default font setting
dFont = ('Open Sans', 50, 'bold')
```

Continued on the next page...

Continuation of code

```python
while True:
    #check for stat to rewrite time lap
    if stat:
        current_loop.clear()
    current_loop.write("Current: " +
str(current), font=dFont)
    #clock counter loop
    for second in range(vid_length):
        #if 6 tens or 60 seconds aka one minute,
        #increment minutes variable by one and
        #replace tens second with 0 to clear
        if lapsed_tensSeconds == 6:
            lapsed_tensSeconds = 0
            lapsed_seconds = 0
            lapsed_minutes += 1

        #write current time including minutes,
        #tens of seconds, and seconds
        clock_counter.write("Time Lapsed: {}:{}
{}" .format(lapsed_minutes, lapsed_tensSeconds,
lapsed_seconds), font=dFont)
        lapsed_seconds += 1
  #if seconds == 10, change variable to 0 and
  #increment tens seconds by one to clear
        if lapsed_seconds == 10:
            lapsed_seconds = 0
            lapsed_tensSeconds += 1
        wait(1)
        clock_counter.clear()
  #after one time lap, increment current by one
  #and reset clock
    current += 1
    lapsed_seconds = 0
    lapsed_tensSeconds = 0
    lapsed_minutes = 0
    clock_counter.clear()
    stat = True
  #end of code
```

Functions and methods used in this book

Global Python Functions

input()

Takes a string parameter. Pauses the program and waits for a user input data. Returns the input data.

Usage:

newinput = input(string)

len()

Measures the length of a string. Requires a string parameter. Does not use dot notation. Returns an integer.

Usage:

length = len(string)

print()

Takes a string parameter. Prints out any printable data; string, numeric, or collection of data.

Usage:

print(string)

String Methods

For the following methods a string variable named "string" is used as an example.

capitalize()

Capitalizes the first letter of the first word in the string. Returns the modified string.

Usage:

newstring = string.capitalize()

count()

Returns the number of characters in the string including spaces.

Usage:

number = string.count()

find()
Returns the index number of a certain letter in the string as defined by the parameter. Takes one parameter.
      Usage:
             index = string.find('w')

isalpha()
Checks if the string is alphanumeric. Returns either True or False.
      Usage:
             status = string.isalpha()

isdigit()
Checks if the string is numeric. Returns either True or False.
      Usage:
             status = string.isdigit()

lower()
Converts all letters to lowercase. Returns a string of lowercase letters.
      Usage:
             lowstring = string.lower()

replace()
Replaces a letter in a string. Requires two parameters. First parameter defines the letter to be replaced. Second parameter defines the letter to replace. Returns the modified string.
      Usage:
             newstring = string.replace('a', 'x')

upper()
Converts all letters to uppercase. Returns a string of uppercase letters.
      Usage:
             upstring = string.upper()

List Methods

For the following methods a list variable named "mylist" is used as an example.

append()
Adds an element to the end of the list. Requires one parameter.
> Usage:
>> mylist.append('Ferrari')

clear()
Removes all elements of the list. No parameter required.
> Usage:
>> mylist.clear()

del
Removes an item from a list at a given index. Does not require dot notation.
> Usage:
>> del mylist[8]

insert()
Inserts an item at a given index. Existing items will be moved over. Requires two parameters --- index number and item.
> Usage:
>> mylist.insert(4, 'Bugatti')

pop()
Removes an element from the list at a specified index. Requires an index parameter.
Usage:
> mylist.pop(5)

remove()
Removes a specified element from the list. Requires a string parameter.
Usage:
> mylist.remove('Bentley')

reverse()
Reverses the order of the list.
>> Usage:
>>>> mylist.reverse()

Set Methods

For the following methods a set variable named "myset" is used as an example.

add()
Adds an element to the set. Requires a parameter.
>> Usage:
>>>> myset.add('Porsche')

remove()
Removes an element from the set. Requires a parameter.
>> Usage:
>>>> myset.remove('Chevrolet')

discard()
Discards an element from the set. Requires a parameter.
>> Usage:
>>>> myset.discard('Lamborghini')

clear()
Removes all elements from the set. No parameter required.
>> Usage:
>>>> myset.clear()

Type Casting Functions

float()
Converts data into a float type. Requires one parameter. Returns a float number.
>> Usage:
>>>> myfloat = float(3445)

int()
Converts data into an integer type. Requires one parameter. Returns an integer number.
> Usage:
>> myinteger = int(3.141518)

str()
Converts data into string. Requires one parameter. Returns the string.
> Usage:
>> mystring = str(2039660305)

Turtle Object Methods

For the following methods a turtle object named "myturtle" is used as an example.

back()
Moves the turtle object back by a number of pixels. Requires a parameter.
> Usage:
>> myturtle.back(195)

begin_fill()
Starts the process of filling the shape with color. No parameter required.
> Usage:
>> myturtle.begin_fill()

bgcolor()
Defines the background color of the Python Turtle Graphics screen. Uses a color parameter. Requires the Screen() object.
> Usage:
>> myturtle.Screen().bgcolor('light green')

color()
Defines the color of the turtle object. Requires a parameter.
> Usage:
>> myturtle.color('red')

colormode()
Defines the color mode for using color. Uses a parameter. Requires the Screen() object.
> Usage:
>> myturtle.Screen().colormode(255)

circle()
Draws a circle. Requires three parameters: radius, degrees, steps.
> Usage:
>> myturtle.circle(55, 360, 30)

clear()
Erases whatever is drawn or written on the Python Turtle Graphics screen. No parameter required.
> Usage:
>> myturtle.clear()

end_fill()
Ends the process of filling the shape with color. No parameter required.
> Usage:
>> myturtle.end_fill()

fillcolor()
Defines the color to fill a shape. Requires a color parameter.
> Usage:
>> myturtle.fillcolor('red')

forward()
Moves the turtle object forward by a number of pixels. Requires an integer parameter.
> Usage:
>> myturtle.forward(255)

hideturtle()
Hides the turtle object. No parameter required.
> Usage:
>> myturtle.hideturtle()

ht()

Hides the turtle object. Short of *hideturtle()*. No parameter required.
>> Usage:
>>>> myturtle.ht()

left()

Turns the turtle object to the left by a given degree. Requires one integer parameter.
>> Usage:
>>>> my turtle.left(45)

pencolor()

Defines the color of the outline. Requires a parameter.
>> Usage:
>> myturtle.pencolor('yellow')

penup()

"Lifts the pen up". Hides the line (or trail) drawn by the turtle when moving.
>> Usage:
>>>> myturtle.penup()

pensize()

Defines the size of the line or "trail" being drawn. Requires one parameter.
>> Usage:
>>>> myturtle.pensize(65)

resizemode()

Resets the size of the turtle object to default. Requires one parameter.
>> Usage:
>>>> myturtle.resizemode('auto')

right()

Turns the turtle object to the right by a given degree. Requires one parameter.
>> Usage:
>>>> myturtle.right(90)

setposition()
Places the turtle object at the given pixel coordinates. Requires two parameters: x and y.

> Usage:
>> myturtle.setposition(350, 275)

setup()
Defines the size of the Python Turtle Graphics window. Requires two parameters: height, width.

> Usage:
>> myturtle.setup(400, 500)

shape()
Defines the actual shape of the turtle object. Requires one parameter.

> Usage:
>> myturtle.shape('turtle')

stamp()
Stamps or imprints the turtle object's shape on the Python Turtle Graphics screen. No parameter required.

> Usage:
>> myturtle.stamp()

Turtle()
The object used when creating a new instance or copy.

> Usage:
>> new_turtle = turtle.Turtle()

turtlesize()
Defines the size of the turtle object. Requires three parameters: height, width, outline.

> Usage:
>> myturtle.turtlesize(15, 15, 3)

write()
Writes a text on the Python Turtle Graphics screen. Requires a string parameter.
> Usage:
>> myturtle.write("Hello universe!")

xcor()
Returns the x coordinate of the turtle object's current position.
> Usage:
>> xposition = myturtle.xcor()

ycor()
Returns the y coordinate of the turtle object's current position.
> Usage:
>> yposition = myturtle.ycor()

© Permission to print from Yzabella Latorilla

References

Websites

www.python.org
>The source of Python compiler.

www.online-python.org
>Online Python editor and compiler.

www.realpython.com
>Tutorials

www.w3schools.com/python/
>Tutorials

www.tutorialspoint.com/python/index.htm
>Tutorials

www.learnpython.org
>Interactive tutorials

Books

Learning Python, 5th Edition by Mark Lutze

Python Programming for Beginners by AMZ publishing

Head First Python: A Brain-Friendly Guide by Paul Barry

Coding for Kids: Python by Adrienne Tacke

Python (2nd Edition) by Jamie Chan

Python for Beginners: A crash course by Brady Ellison

Acknowledgements

I thank my parents for giving me the time and
resources I needed to write this book. Their support
and encouragement were most invaluable
in reaching my goal.

I thank my sister, Yzabella, for providing the
cover art and illustrations in the book.
Her art makes learning fun and amusing.

I thank Noel Villamor in Australia for providing
additional technical help.

Index

#, 41 - 2

A
add(), 84
and, 61
append(), 77
args, 153
argument, 153, 156
array, 70
assignment, 56

B
back(), 130
backslash, 45
base 10, 122
base 16, 122
begin_fill(), 138
bit, 121
bgcolor(), 117-8
brackets, 70, 82, 86
   square, 70
   curly, 82, 86
Boolean, 57, 61-2, 70
byte, 121

C
camelCase, 49
capitalize(), 68
casting, type, 107-8
character, 45
circle(), 141
class, 47
clear(), 78, 85, 141

code
   block, 110
   color coding, 37-8
   table, 36-7
color
   RGB, 120
   hexadecimal, 122
   filling a shape, 138
colormode(), 121
comparison, 57
concatenation, 50
coordinates, 148
colon, 86, 93, 108-12, 150
color, 119-123
color(), 124
condition, 111
   Boolean, 100
constructor, 81
comment, 41
count(), 69
counter, 111

D
data
   type, 47
   typecasting, 107-8
decision, 91-104
   complex, 102-3
   conditions, 92
   making, 91
def, 150-2
degree, 142
del, 76

dictionary, 85-6
   key:value pair, 85
discard(), 84
dot notation, 66-9
download Python, 10, 17
   on MacOS, 10-11
   on Windows, 17-8
duplicates, 72, 84

E
element, 71, 83
elif, 97-8
else, 98
end_fill(), 139
escape, 45
extent, 141

F
False, 57, 61-2
file, 26-30
   creating, 26-7
   saving, 27-8
   running, 29-30
   recent, 32
fillcolor(), 138
find(), 68
float, 54
flowchart, 91
for, 108
forward(), 130
function, 149-156
   calling, 151
   creating, 150
   def, 150-1
   name, 150
   parameter, 156
   return, 156

H
hashtag, 41-2
hex, 122
hexadecimal, 122
ht(), 136
hideturtle(), 136

I
IDLE, 20, 39-41
   using, 20
   on MacOS, 21
   on Windows, 23
   shell, 24
if, 93-5
   else, 96
   elif, 97-8
import, 115, 137, 140, 144
in, 79
indexed, 71
input
   user, 65-6
insert(), 78
install Python, 13, 18
   MacOS, 13-6
   Windows, 18-9
int, 47
integer, 54
isalpha(), 69
isdigit(), 68
iteration
   basic, 100
   range, 110
   step, 100

K

key, 85

keyboard, shortcuts, 31

L

left(), 131

len(), 67

list, 70-80

  del, 76

  index, negative, 75

  index, skip, 75

  methods, 77-8

  mutable, 76

  slicing, 73-4

list(), 81

logical, 99, 102

loop, 108-112

  constructing, 109, 110

  for loop, 108-11

  iterating, 109

  incrementing, 111

  range iteration, 110

  step iteration, 100

  while loop, 111-2

lower(), 68

M

method

  set, 84-5

  string, 66-9

  list, 77-8

membership, 99, 104

module, 115-9

multiline, 45-6

N

not, 62

  not in, 80

notation, 66-9

numbers, 54

numeric, 54

O

object, 117

  screen, 117

  turtle, 117

operator, 54-62

  arithmetic, 55

  assignment, 56

  combining, 62

  comparison, 57

  logical, 61-2

  membership, 79-80

or, 61

P

parameter, 110, 156

parentheses, 80

pascalCase, 49

PEMDAS, 55

pen, 133-140

  making, 133

  pencolor(), 125

  pensize(), 147

  penup(), 131, 143

pop(), 78

print(), 24-5

program, running, 30

Python, why, 10

  download, 10

  install, 10

Q

quotes, 45

R

radius, 141
random module, 162
range, 73, 110
    range(), 109-10
    slice, 73
remove(), 84
replace(), 69
resizemode(), 128
return, 156
reusability, 149
RGB, 120
    limit, 121
right(), 131
reverse(), 78
run, a program, 30

S

set, 82-5
    methods, 84
    add(), 84
    clear(), 85
    discard(), 84
    remove(), 84
setposition()
setup(), 117
Screen()
    bgcolor(), 117-8
    colormode(), 121
screenshots, 35
shape(), 116
Shell, 20-5
    IDLE, 24

shortcuts, keyboard, 31
sleep(), 163
slice, 73
stamp(), 143-4
steps, 141
str, 47
string, 40, 50-1
    F-string, 51, 66
    methods, 66-9
    dot notation, 66-7
    with user input, 69
styling, 49
syntax, 43-6
    escape, multilines, 45-6
SyntaxError, 43

T

time module, 162
True, 57, 61-2
tuple, 80-2
    constructors, 81
tuple(), 81
turtle, 115-9
    back(), 130
    forward(), 130
    import, 115
    left(), 131
    outline, 128-9
    pencolor(), 125
    resizemode(), 128
    right(), 131
    shape(), 116
    Turtle(), 133
    turtlesize(), 127
type, 47
    casting, 107-8

U

underscore, 49

user, input, 65-6

upper(), 66

V

variable, 48-50, 111

   in strings, 50-1

   incrementing, 111

   counter, 111

value, 85, 153-6

W

while loop, 111-2

write(), 141

X

xcor(), 148

Y

ycor(), 148

Notes

Notes

Notes

Notes

Notes

About the Author

Jason Latorilla was born in the USA. He wrote this book at age 13 when he was in middle school.

He loves reading books specially about world history and geography in addition to learning computer coding.

www.ingramcontent.com/pod-product-compliance
Lightning Source LLC
LaVergne TN
LVHW051639050326
832903LV00022B/809